COMMENTARY ON DANIEL

St. Jerome

Doctor of the Church

Translated from the Latin by

Gleason L. Archer

Dalcassian Publishing Co

Library of Congress Cataloging-in-Publication Data

Prologue

Porphyry wrote his twelfth book against the prophecy of Daniel, (A) denying that it was composed by the person to whom it is ascribed in its title, but rather by some individual living in Judaea at the time of the Antiochus who was surnamed Epiphanes. He furthermore alleged that "Daniel" did not foretell the future so much as he related the past, and lastly that whatever he spoke of up till the time of Antiochus contained authentic history, whereas anything he may have conjectured beyond that point was false, inasmuch as he would not have foreknown the future. Eusebius, Bishop of Caesarea, made a most able reply to these allegations in three volumes, that is, the eighteenth, nineteenth, and twentieth. Appollinarius did likewise, in a single large book, namely his twenty-sixth. (B) Prior to these authors Methodius made a partial reply.

But inasmuch as it is not our purpose to make answer to the false accusations of an adversary, a task requiring lengthy discussion, but rather to treat of the actual content of the prophet's message for the benefit of us who are Christians, I wish to stress in my preface this fact, that none of the prophets has so clearly spoken concerning Christ as has this prophet Daniel. For not only did he assert that He would come, a prediction common to the other prophets as well, but also he set forth the very time at which He would come. Moreover he went through the various kings in order, stated the actual number of years involved, and announced beforehand the clearest signs of events to come. And because Porphyry saw that all these things had been fulfilled and could not deny that they had taken place, he overcame this evidence of historical accuracy by taking refuge in this evasion, contending that whatever is foretold concerning Antichrist at the end of the world was actually fulfilled in the reign of Antiochus Epiphanes, because of certain similarities to things which took place at his time. But this very attack testifies to Daniel's accuracy. For so striking was the reliability of what the prophet foretold, that he could not appear to unbelievers as a predicter of the future, but rather a narrator of things already past. And so wherever occasion arises in the course of explaining this volume, I shall attempt briefly to answer his malicious charge, and to controvert by simple explanation the philosophical skill, or rather the worldly malice, by which he strives to subvert the truth and by specious legerdemain to remove that which is so apparent to our eyes.

I would therefore beseech you, Pammachius, as a foremost lover of learning, and Marcella, as an outstanding examplar of Roman virtue, men who are bound together by faith and blood, to lend aid to my efforts by your prayers, in order that our Lord and Savior might in His own cause and by His mind make answer through my mouth. For it is He who says to the prophet, "Open thy mouth and I will fill it" (Psalm 80:11). For if He admonishes us, when we have been hailed before judges and tribunals, not to ponder what answer we are to give to them (Luke 12), how much more is He able to carry on His own war against blaspheming adversaries and through His servants to vanquish them? For this reason a great number of the Psalms also contain that Hebrew expression, lamanasse1, rendered by the Septuagint as "To the end," but which rather is to be understood as "For victory!" For Aquila construed it as to nikopoio, that is, "To Him who grants the victory." Symmachus renders it as epinikion which properly signifies "Triumph and the palm of victory."

But among other things we should recognize that Porphyry makes this objection to us concerning the Book of Daniel, that it is clearly a forgery not to be considered as belonging to the Hebrew Scriptures but an invention composed in Greek. This he deduces from the fact that in the story of Susanna, where Daniel is speaking to the elders, we find the expressions, "To split from the mastic tree" (apo tou skhinou skhisai) and to saw from the evergreen oak (kai apo tou prinou prisai), (D) a wordplay appropriate to Greek rather than to Hebrew. But both Eusebius and Apollinarius have answered him after the same tenor, that the stories of

Susanna and of Bel and the Dragon are not contained in the Hebrew, but rather they constitute a part of the prophecy of Habakkuk, the son of Jesus of the tribe of Levi. Just as we find in the title of that same story of Bel, according to the Septuagint, "There was a certain priest named Daniel, the son of Abda, an intimate of the King of Babylon." And yet Holy Scripture testifies that Daniel and the three Hebrew children were of the tribe of Judah. For this same reason when I was translating Daniel many years ago, I noted these visions with a critical symbol, showing that they were not included in the Hebrew. And in this connection I am surprised to be told that certain fault-finders complain that I have on my own initiative truncated the book. After all, both Origen, Eusebius and Apollinarius, and other outstanding churchmen and teachers of Greece acknowledge that, as I have said, these visions are not found amongst the Hebrews, and that therefore they are not obliged to answer to Porphyry for these portions which exhibit no authority as Holy Scripture.

I also wish to emphasize to the reader the fact that it was not according to the Septuagint version but according to the version of Theodotion himself that the churches publicly read Daniel. (A) And Theodotion, at any rate, was an unbeliever subsequent to the advent of Christ, although some assert that he was an Ebionite which is another variety of Jew. But even Origen in his Vulgate edition (of the Greek Old Testament) placed asterisks around the work of Theodotion, indicating that the material added was missing (in the Septuagint), whereas on the other hand he prefixed obeli (i.e., diacritical marks) to some of the verses, distinguishing thereby whatever was additional material (not contained in the Hebrew). And since all the churches of Christ, whether belonging to the Greek-speaking territory or the Latin, the Syrian or the Egyptian, publicly read this edition with its asterisks and obeli, let the hostile-minded not begrudge my labor, because I wanted our (Latin-speaking) people to have what the Greek-speaking peoples habitually read publicly in the regions of Aquila and Symmachus. And if the Greeks do not for all their wealth of learning despise the scholarly work of Jews, why should poverty-stricken Latins look down upon a man who is a Christian? And if my product seems unsatisfactory, at least my good intentions should be recognized.

But now it is time for us to unfold the words of the prophet himself, not following our usual custom of setting everything forth in detail with an accompanying detailed discussion (the procedure followed in our commentary on the Twelve Minor Prophets), but rather employing a certain brevity and inserting at intervals an explanation of only those things which are obscure. In this way we hope to avoid tiring the reader with an innumerable abundance of books. And yet to understand the final portions of Daniel a detailed investigation of Greek history is necessary, that is to say, such authorities as (B) Sutorius, Callinicus, Diodorus, Hieronymus, Polybius, Posidonius, Claudius, Theon, and Andronycus surnamed Alipius, historians whom Porphyry claims to have followed, Josephus also and those whom he cites, and especially our own historian, Livy, and Pompeius Trogus, and Justinus. All these men narrate the history involved in Daniel's final vision, carrying it beyond the time of Alexander to the days of Caesar Augustus in their description of the Syrian and Egyptian wars, i.e., those of Seleucus, Antiochus, and the Ptolemies. And if we are compelled from time to time to make mention of profane literature and speak of matters therein contained which we have formerly failed to mention, it is not by personal preference but by stark necessity, so to speak, in order to prove that those things which were foretold by the holy prophets many centuries before are actually contained in the written records of both the Greeks and Romans and of other peoples as well.

CHAPTER ONE

Verse 1. "In the third year of the reign of Joacim (Jehoiakim) king of Judah, Nebuchadnezzar king of Babylon came to Jerusalem and besieged it." Jehoiakim, son of the Josiah in whose thirteenth regnal year Jeremiah began to prophesy, and under whom the woman Hulda prophesied, was the same man as was called by the other name of Eliakim, and reigned over the tribes of Judah and Jerusalem eleven years. His son Jehoiachin [misprinted "Joachim" for "Joachin"; cf. IV Reg. 24:6 in the Vulgate] surnamed Jeconiah, followed him in the kingship, and on the tenth day of the third month of his reign he was taken captive by Nebuchadnezzar's generals and brought to Babylon. In his place his paternal uncle Zedekiah, a son of Josiah, was appointed king, and in his eleventh year Jerusalem was captured and destroyed. Let no one therefore imagine that the Jehoiakim in the beginning of Daniel is the same person as the one who is spelled Jehoiachin [Lat. Joachin] in the commencement of Ezekiel. For the latter has "-chin" as its final syllable, whereas the former has "-kim." And it is for this reason that in the Gospel according to Matthew there seems to be a generation missing, because the second group of fourteen, (A) extending to the time of Jehoiakim, ends with a son of Josiah, and the third group begins with Jehoiachin, son of Jehoiakim. Being ignorant of this factor, Porphyry formulated a slander against the Church which only revealed his own ignorance, as he tried to prove the evangelist Matthew guilty of error.

Verse 2. "And the Lord gave Jehoiakim king of Judah into his hand." (B) The fact that Jehoiachim is recorded to have been given over shows that it was not a victory for the might of his enemies but rather it was of the will of the Lord. "...and some of the vessels of the house of God, and he brought them to the land of Shinar (C) to the house of his god, and he conveyed them into the treasure house of his god" (Gen. 11). The land of Shinar is a region of Babylon in which the plain of Dura was located, and also the tower which those who had migrated from the East attempted to build up to heaven. From this circumstance and from the confusion of tongues the region received the name Babylon, which, translated into our language, means "confusion." At the same time it ought to be noted, by way of spiritual interpretation [anagogen], that the king of Babylon was not able to transport all of the vessels of God, and place them in the idol-house which he had built himself, but only a part of the vessels of God's house. By these vessels we are to understand the dogmas of truth. For if you go through all of the works of the philosophers, you will necessarily find in them some portion of the vessels of God. For example, you will find in Plato that God is the fashioner of the universe, in Zeno the chief of the Stoics, that there are inhabitants in the infernal regions and that souls are immortal, and that honor is the one (true) good. But because the philosophers combine truth with error and corrupt the good of nature with many evils, for that reason they are recorded to have captured only a portion of the vessels of God's house, and not all of them in their completeness and perfection. Verse 3. "And the king said to Ashpenaz the overseer of his eunuchs, (D) that he should out of the number of the children of Israel and, of the royal seed and (the seed of) the rulers [tyrannorum, Jer.'s rendering of Heb. partemim, "nobles"] bring in some young lads who were free from all blemish." Instead of Ashpenaz ("Asphanez") I found Abriesdri written in the Vulgate [i.e., the LXX] edition. For the word phorlhommin which Theodotion uses, the Septuagint and Aquila translated "the chosen ones," whereas Symmachus rendered "Parthians," understanding it as the name of a nation instead of a common noun. This is in disagreement with the Hebrew edition as it is accurately read; I have translated it as "rulers," especially because it is preceded by the words "of the seed royal." From this passage the Hebrews think that Daniel, Hananiah, Mishael, and Azariah were eunuchs, thus fulfilling that prophecy which is spoken by Isaiah regarding Hezekiah: "And they shall take of thy seed and make eunuchs of them in the house of the king (E) of Babylon" (Isa. 37: 7). If however they were of the seed royal, there is no doubt but what they were of the line of David. But perhaps the following words are opposed to this interpretation: "... lads, or youths, who were free from all blemish, in order that he might teach them the literature and language of the

Chaldeans." Philo supposes that Chaldee is the same thing as the Hebrew language, because Abraham came from the Chaldeans. But if we accept this we must ask how the Hebrew lads could now be bidden to be taught a language which they already knew; unless, perchance, we should say, as some believe, that Abraham was acquainted with two languages.

Verse 7. "And the overseer of the eunuchs imposed names upon them, calling Daniel Belteshazzar (Balthasar), and Hananiah Shadrach, and Mishael Meshach, and Azariah Abednego." It was not only the overseer or master of the eunuchs (as others have rendered it, the "chief-eunuch") who changed the names of saints, but also Pharaoh called Joseph in Egypt (Gen. 41) (F) Somtonphanec [Heb.: Zaphenath-paaneah], for neither of them wished them to have Jewish names in the land of captivity. Wherefore the prophet says in the Psalm: "How shall we sing the Lord's song in a strange land?" (Ps. 136:4). Furthermore the Lord Himself changes names benignly, and on the basis of events imposes names of special significance, so as to call Abram Abraham, and Sarai Sarah (Gen. 17). Also in the Gospel, the former Simon received the name of Peter (Mark 3), (A) and the sons of Zebedee are called "sons of thunder"----which is not boanerges, as most people suppose, but is more correctly read benereem [a reading for which there is no manuscript support, but which would be the Hebrew for "sons of thunder"].

Verse 8. "Daniel, however, purposed in his heart that he would not be defiled by food from the king's table, nor by the wine which he drank, and he asked the chief of the eunuchs that he might not be polluted." He who would not eat or drink of the king's food or wine lest he be denied (especially if he should be aware that the wisdom and teaching of the Babylonians is mistaken), would never consent to utter what was wrong. On the contrary they [i.e., the Hebrew youths] speak it forth, not that they may follow it themselves, but in order to pass judgment upon it and refute it. Just as anyone would expose himself to ridicule if he being untrained in mathematics should desire to write in confutation of mathematicians, or, being ignorant of the teachings of philosophers should desire to write in opposition to philosophers. Hence they [i.e., the Hebrew youths] study the teaching of the Chaldeans with the same intention as Moses studied the wisdom (B) of the Egyptians.

Verse 9. "God gave Daniel favor and compassion in the sight of the prince of eunuchs. . . . " He who was taken into captivity on account of the sins of his forebears received an immediate recompense for the magnitude of his own virtues. For he had purposed in his heart that he would not be denied by food from the king's table, and preferred humble fare to royal delicacies; therefore, by the bounteous bestowal of the Lord he received favor and compassion in the sight of the prince of the eunuchs. By this we may understand that if ever under pressing circumstances holy men are loved by unbelievers, it is a matter of the mercy of God, not of the goodness of perverted men.

Verse 12. "I beg thee, try us thy servants for ten days, (C) and let pulse be given us to eat and water to drink." His faith was so incredibly great that he not only promised he would be in good flesh by eating the humbler food, but he even set a time-limit. Therefore, it was not a matter of temerity but of faith, for the sake of which he despised the sumptuous fare of the king.

Verse 17. "But God gave these lads knowledge and learning in every book and branch of wisdom, and He gave to Daniel besides an understanding of all visions and dreams." Note that God is said to have given the holy lads knowledge and learning in secular literature, in every book and branch of wisdom. Symmachus rendered this by "grammatical art," implying that they understood everything they read, and by the Spirit of God could make a judgment concerning the lore of the Chaldeans. But Daniel had an outstanding gift over and above the three lads, in that he could astutely discern the significance of visions and dreams in which things to come are shown forth by means of certain symbols and mysteries. Therefore, that which others saw only in a shadowy appearance he could perceive clearly with the eyes of his understanding.

Verse 18. "Therefore, when the days had been completed at the end of which the king had bidden them to be presented to him, the chief of the eunuchs presented them in the presence of Nebuchadnezzar." By the "completed days" understand the period of three years which the king had appointed so that after they had been nourished and trained for three years, they should then stand in the presence of the king.

Verse 20. "And every word of wisdom and understanding the king inquired of them, he found it in them ten times as great as all the soothsayers and magicians put together who were to be found in his entire realm." For "soothsayers" and "magicians" the Vulgate edition [i.e., of the Septuagint] translated "sophists" and "philosophers"----terms to be understood not in the sense of the philosophy and sophistic erudition which Greek learning holds forth, but rather in the sense of the lore of a barbarian people, which the Chaldeans pursue as philosophy even to this day.

"Daniel therefore continued unto the first year of Cyrus the king." In the later discussion, we shall explain how it was that Daniel who is here described as having continued till the first year of king Cyrus afterwards held office in the third year of that same Cyrus and is even recorded to have lived in the first year of Darius.

CHAPTER TWO
Verse 1. "In the second year of the reign of Nebuchadnezzar, Nebuchadnezzar saw a dream and his spirit was terrified, and his dream fled from him." If the three lads had entered before him at the end of three years, as he himself had commanded, how is it that he is now said to have seen the dream in the second year of his reign? The Hebrews solve the difficulty in this way, that the second year refers here to his reign over all the barbarian nations, not only Judah and the Chaldeans, but also the Assyrians and Egyptians, and the Moabites and the rest of the nations which by the permission of God he had conquered. For this reason Josephus also writes in the tenth book of the Antiquities: After the second year from the devastation of Egypt Nebuchadnezzar beheld a marvelous dream, and "his spirit was terrified and his dream fled from him." The impious king beheld a dream concerning things to come, in order that he might give glory to God after the holy man had interpreted what he had seen, and that great consolation might be afforded the captive (Jews) and those who still served God in their captive state. We read this same thing in the case of Pharaoh, not because Pharaoh and Nebuchadnezzar deserved to behold visions, but in order that Joseph and Daniel might appear as deserving of preference over all other men because of their gift of interpretation.

Verse 2. "Wherefore the king commanded that the soothsayers, the magi, the charmers, and the Chaldeans show the king his dream. And when they came, they stood in the presence of the king." Those whom we have translated as "soothsayers" (harioli) others have rendered as epaoidoi, that is, "enchanters." Well then, it seems to me that enchanters are people who perform a thing by means of words; magi are those who pursue individual lines (D) of philosophic enquiry; charmers are those who employ blood and animal sacrifices and often have contact with corpses. Furthermore the term "astrologers" [or nativity-casters, genethlialogoi] among the Chaldeans signifies, I believe, what the common people call mathematicians. But common usage and ordinary conversation understands the term magi as wicked enchanters (E). Yet they were regarded differently among their own nation, inasmuch as they were the philosophers of the Chaldeans, and even the kings and princes of this same nation do all they can to acquire a knowledge of this science. Wherefore also it was they who first at the nativity of our Lord and Savior learned of his birth, and who came to holy Bethlehem and adored the child, under the guidance of the star which shone above them (Matt. 2).

Verse 3. "And the king said to them, 'I have seen a dream, and from the confusion of my mind I do not know what I have seen.' " There remained in the king's heart only a shadow, so to speak, or a mere echo or trace of the dream, with the result that if others should retell it to him, he would be able to recall what he had seen, and they would certainly not be deceiving him with lies.

Verse 4. "The Chaldeans replied to the king in Syriac." (A) Up to this point what we have read has been recounted in Hebrew. From this point on until the vision of the third year of King Balthasar [Belshazzar] which Daniel saw in Susa, the account is written in Hebrew characters, to be sure, but in the Chaldee language, which he here calls Syriac.

Verse 5. "If you do not show me the vision and its interpretation, ye shall perish and your homes shall be confiscated . ..." He threatened punishment and offered rewards, in order that if they should be able to tell him the dream, he might therefore believe also that which was uncertain, namely the meaning of the dream. But if they should be unable to tell the king what he in his mental confusion could not recall, they would also lose claim to trustworthiness in the interpretation they might give. At last there follows the statement:

Verses 9, 10. "Therefore tell me the dream, that I may be certain that ye are giving me its true interpretation. (B) The Chaldeans therefore made this reply in the king's presence: 'There is no man on earth who would be able to fulfil what thou hast spoken, O king!'" The magi confess, along with the soothsayers----and all secular learning concurs----that foreknowledge of the future lies not in man's province but in God's. By this test it is proved that the prophets who proclaimed things to come spoke by the Spirit of God.

Verses 12, 13. "And when he had heard this, the king in a furious rage gave orders that all the wise men of Babylon should be slain. And when the decree went forth, the wise men were being slaughtered. ..." (C) The Hebrews raise the question of why Daniel and the three lads did not enter before the king along with the other wise men, and why they were ordered to be slain with the rest when the decree was issued. They have explained the difficulty in this way, by saying that at that time, when the king was promising rewards and gifts and great honor, they did not care to go before him, lest they should appear to be shamelessly grasping after the wealth and honor of the Chaldeans. Or else it was undoubtedly true that the Chaldeans themselves, being envious of the Jews' reputation and learning, entered alone before the king, as if to obtain the rewards by themselves. Afterwards they were perfectly willing to have those whom they had denied any hope of glory to share in a common peril.

Verse 15. "And he inquired of him who had received authority from the king as to why so cruel a decree had gone forth from the presence of the king." Knowing that Daniel and the three youths possessed a knowledge and intelligence tenfold as great as that of all the soothsayers of Chaldea put together, the Chaldeans concealed from them the king's inquiry, lest they should receive preference over them in the matter of interpreting the dream. On this account Daniel inquired concerning the cruelty of the decree, being ignorant of the cause of his own peril.

Verses 16, 17. "Therefore (D) when Arioch had explained the matter to Daniel, Daniel entered in and asked the king to grant him some time for the disclosure of the solution to the king. And he entered his home and disclosed the affair to his comrades, Hananiah, Mishael, and Azariah...." Daniel requested time, not that he might investigate secret things by the clever application of his intellect, but that he might beseech the Lord of Secrets. And for that reason he engaged Hananiah, Mishael, and Azariah to join with him in supplication, to avoid the appearance of presuming upon his own merit alone, and to the end that those involved in a common danger might engage in common prayer.

Verse 19. "And Daniel blessed the God of heaven, and spoke, saying,. ..." In contrast to those who occupy themselves with this world and delude the earthly minded with demonic arts and illusions, Daniel blessed the God of heaven. For the gods who did not create heaven and earth will pass away.

Verse 21. "And it is He who changes times and seasons, who transfers kingdoms and establishes kingdoms." Let us not marvel, therefore, whenever we see kings and empires succeed one another, for it is by the will of God that they are governed, altered, and terminated. And the cases of individuals are well known to Him who founded all things. He often permits wicked kings to arise in order that they may in their wickedness punish the wicked. At the same time by indirect suggestion and general discussion he prepares the reader for the fact that the dream Nebuchadnezzar saw was concerned with the change and succession of empires. "He gives wisdom to the wise and knowledge to those who acquire learning." This accords with the scripture: "The wise man will hear and increase his wisdom" (Prov. 1:5). "For he who has, to him it shall be given" (Matt. 25:29). A soul which cherishes an ardent love of wisdom is freely infilled by the Spirit of God. But wisdom will never penetrate a perverse soul (Wisdom 3).

Verse 22. "It is He who reveals deep and hidden things, and He knows what is placed in the darkness, and with Him is the light." A man to whom God makes profound revelations and who can say, "O the depth of the riches of the knowledge and wisdom of God!" (Rom. 11:33), he it is who by the indwelling Spirit probes even into the deep things of God, and digs the deepest of wells in the depths of his soul. He is a man who has stirred up the whole earth, which is wont to conceal the deep waters, and he observes the command of God, saying: "Drink water from thy vessels and from the spring of thy wells" (Prov. 5:15). As for the words which follow, "He knows what is placed in the darkness, and with Him is the light," the darkness signifies ignorance, and the light signifies knowledge and learning. Therefore as wrong cannot hide God away, so right encompasses and surrounds Him. Or else we should interpret the words to mean all the dark mysteries and deep things (concerning God), according to what we read in Proverbs: "He understands also the parable and the dark saying." This in turn is equivalent to what we read in the Psalms: "Dark waters in the clouds of the sky" (Ps. 17:12). For one who ascends to the heights and forsakes the things of earth, and like the birds themselves seeks after the most rarified atmosphere and everything ethereal, he becomes like a cloud to which the truth of God penetrates and which habitually showers rain upon the saints. Replete with a plenitude of knowledge, he contains in his breast many dark waters enveloped with deep darkness, a darkness which only Moses can penetrate (Ex. 23) and speak with God face to face, of Whom the Scripture says: "He hath made darkness His hiding-place" (Ps. 17:12).

Verse 23. "I confess Thee, O god of my fathers (A), and I praise Thee because Thou hast granted me wisdom and strength." Lest it should seem to be an achievement of his own deserving, Daniel assigns it to the righteousness of his forefathers and to the faithfulness of God, Who takes pity upon their posterity even in exile.

"And now Thou hast shown me that for which we petitioned Thee. ..." That which the four of them had asked for is disclosed to the one, for the twofold purpose that he might escape any temptation to pride, on the ground of having obtained the request by himself, and also that he might render thanksgiving because he alone heard the secret of the dream.

Verse 24. "Destroy not the wise men of Babylon. Take me in before the king and I will set forth the explanation to the king. ..." He follows the example of the clemency of God, who intercedes in behalf of his persecutors, and is unwilling that those men should perish on whose account he himself had been threatened with death.

Verse 25. "I have found a man who belongs to the children of the captivity of Judah and who will set forth the explanation to the king." He credits his own diligence with what God's grace has bestowed, and he claims that he himself has done the finding, when actually Daniel had applied to him of his own volition that he might be presented to the king. This instance manifests the habitual (B) reaction of messengers, for when they have good news to report, they wish it to appear their own doing. But the man who undertakes the explanation of the dream is certainly going to relate the dream beforehand. And note that Daniel is said to be of the children of Judah, rather than being a priest as the latter part of the story of Bel relates.

Verse 26. "Dost thou truly believe that thou canst show me the dream I have seen...." In framing his inquiry he adheres to logical sequence, so that he first asks for the dream, of which the magi had replied they were ignorant, and afterwards he asks for the interpretation of the dream. The implication is that after he has heard the dream, then he would believe also in the correctness of what was susceptible of varying interpretations.

Verse 27. "As for the secret for which the king is asking, neither the wise men nor the magi nor the soothsayers nor the diviners are able to declare it to the king." In place of diviners (haruspices), as we have rendered it, the Hebrew [sic!] text has Gazareni [actually the Aramaic word is gazerin], which only Symmachus has rendered as (C) sacrificers [thutai], a. class of people whom the Greeks usually call liver-diviners (epatoskopoi), and who inspect the inwards in order to make predictions from them concerning the future. By terming a mystery the category of a revealed dream, Daniel shows that whatever is hidden and unknown by men can still be called a "mystery." Moreover he obviates any evil suspicion on the king's part, lest he should imagine that human cleverness can discover something which is reserved to the knowledge of God alone.

Verse 28. "But there is a God in heaven who reveals mysteries." Therefore it is only in vain that thou inquirest (other MSS have: "that he inquire") of men as to something which is known only to God in heaven. Also, by indirectly drawing Nebuchadnezzar away from the worship of many gods, Daniel directs him to the knowledge of the one (true) God.

"Who hath shown thee, King Nebuchadnezzar, what is going to take place (the Vulg. reads: "the things which are going to take place") in the last times." Avoiding the blemish of adulation but cleaving to the truth, he courteously suggests that it is to the king [God has shown these things], for it was to him that God had revealed secrets concerning what was to occur in the last times. Now either these "last days" are to be reckoned from the time when the dream was revealed to Daniel until the end of the world, or else at least this inference is to be drawn, that the over-all interpretation of the dream applies to that final end when the image (D) and statue beheld [in the dream] is to be ground to powder.

"Thy dream and the visions of thy head upon thy bed were as follows." He does not say, "The visions of thine eyes," lest we should think it was something physical, but rather: "of thy head." "For the eyes of a wise man are in his head" (Eccl. 2:14), that is to say in the princely organ of the heart, just as we read in the Gospel: "Blessed are the pure in heart, for they are ones who shall see God" (Matt. 5:8). Again: "What (E) are ye meditating in your hearts?" (Matt. 9:4). To be sure, other authorities in treating of this chapter [i.e., Matt. 9], conjecture that the authoritative part of the soul (to hegemonikon) lies not in the heart but, as Plato says, in the brain.

Verse 29. "Thou, O king, didst begin to meditate upon thy bed as to what should come to pass hereafter." Instead of the true reading the Septuagint alone inserts the translation "in the last days" after the "hereafter." But if it be read thus, we must inquire quite carefully as to where "last days" have been written; and we would refute those who think the world will never be destroyed. For never would any days be called "the last days" if the world were everlasting. And as for the statement, "Thou, O king, didst begin to meditate," this would indicate the [psychological] motives behind the dream; for it was for this reason that God revealed to him the secrets of the future, because the king himself wished to know what was going to happen. Also, in order that Nebuchadnezzar might marvel at the gracious gift of divine inspiration, he sets forth not only (A) what the king had beheld in the dream, but also what he had thought to himself (beforehand).

"...and He who reveals secrets has shown thee what is to come to pass." The statement which we read in the Gospel, "Who maketh His sun to rise upon the wicked and the good" (Matt. 5:45), we realize to have been fulfilled in the case of Nebuchadnezzar also. For so great was God's mercy that He even revealed to Nebuchadnezzar secrets as to His own mode of government whereby he rules the world. Let us ask those who assert that men's characters belong to one extreme or the other, which character do they understand Nebuchadnezzar to have possessed, the good or the evil? If the good, why is he called an impious man? If the evil (which was certainly the case), why did God show forth His holy secrets to one who was evil and earthly, that is to say, earthen?

Verse 30. "Moreover, this holy secret has not been revealed to me in virtue of any wisdom which inheres in me more than in all living men, but rather that the interpretation might be manifested to the king, and that thou mayest know the thoughts of thine own mind." The king had imagined that cleverness of the human intellect could embrace a knowledge of the future, and for that reason he had ordered the wise men of Babylon to be slain. Daniel therefore makes excuse for those who were unable to speak, and himself avoids the envy of others, lest any should imagine that he had said any of the things he was going to say by virtue of his personal wisdom. But the cause of the prophetic revelation was the earnest desire of the king, who wished to know the future. Consequently, he does honor to the king, because he states that it was for the sake of the king's knowledge that the secrets have been revealed by God. And this fact should be pondered, that dreams in which any coming events are signified and in which truth is shown forth, as it were, through a cloud, are not manifest to the conjectures or dominion of the human mind but to the knowledge of God alone.

Verse 31. "Thou sawest, O king, and behold there was, as it were, a large statue." (B) Instead of "statue," that is a sculptured effigy, the only rendering used by Symmachus, others have translated it as "image," intending by this term to indicate a resemblance to future events. Let us go through the prophetic interpretation, and as we translate Daniel's words (C), let us explain at some length the matters which he briefly states.

"Now thou art the head of gold." "The head of gold," he says "is thou, O king." By this statement it is clear that the first empire, the Babylonian, is compared to the most precious metal, gold.

Verse 39. "And after thee there shall arise another empire inferior to thee, made of silver." (The Vulgate LXX does not include "made of silver.") That is to say, the empire of the Medes and Persians, which bears a resemblance to silver, being inferior to the preceding empire, and superior to that which is to follow.

"And a third empire of bronze (the Vulgate LXX has "made of copper"), which shall rule over the entire earth." This signifies the Alexandrian empire, and that of the Macedonians, and of Alexander's successors. Now this is properly termed brazen, for among all the metals bronze possesses an outstanding resonance and a clear ring, and the blast of a brazen trumpet is heard far and wide, so that it signifies not only the fame and power of the empire but also the eloquence of the Greek language.

Verse 40. "And there shall be a fourth empire like unto iron. Just as iron breaks to pieces and overcomes all else, so it shall break to pieces and shatter all these preceding empires . ..." Now the fourth empire, which clearly refers to the Romans, is the iron empire which breaks in pieces and overcomes all others. But its feet and toes are partly of iron and partly of earthenware, a fact most clearly demonstrated at the present time. For just as there was at the first nothing stronger or hardier than the Roman realm, so also in these last days there is nothing more feeble (D), since we require the assistance of barbarian tribes both in our civil wars and against foreign nations. However, at the final period of all these empires of gold and silver and bronze and iron, a rock (namely, the Lord and Savior) was cut off without hands, that is, without copulation or human seed and by birth from a virgin's womb; and after all the empires had been crushed, He became a great mountain and filled the whole earth. This last the Jews and the impious Porphyry apply to the people of Israel, who they insist will be the strongest power at the end of the ages, and will crush all realms and will rule forever.

Verse 45. "The great God has shown to the king the events which shall hereafter come to pass, and the dream is true and its interpretation is reliable." Daniel again asserts that the revelation of the dream is not a matter of personal merit, but has been granted for the purpose of making the interpretation manifest to the king and of teaching the king that God alone is to be worshipped.

Verse 47. "Then King Nebuchadnezzar fell on his face and worshipped Daniel, and ordered sacrifices and incense to be offered up to him. (E) Therefore the king spoke and said to Daniel." Porphyry falsely impugns this passage on the ground that a very proud king would never worship a mere captive, as if, forsooth, the Lycaonians had not been willing to offer blood sacrifices to Paul and Barnabas on account of the mighty miracles they had wrought. And so there is no need to impute to the Scripture the error of the Gentiles who deem everything above themselves [i.e., superhuman] to be gods, for the Scripture simply is narrating everything as it actually happened. However, we can make this further assertion, that the king himself set forth the reasons for his worship and offering of blood-sacrifices when he said to Daniel:

"Truly thy God is the God of gods and the Lord of kings and a revealer of mysteries, since thou hast been able to disclose this holy secret." And so it was not so much that he was worshipping Daniel as that he was through Daniel worshipping the God who had revealed the holy secrets (F). This is the same thing that we read Alexander the Great, King of the Macedonians, did in the high priesthood of Joaida [i.e., Jaddua]. Or, if this explanation seem unsatisfactory, we shall have to say that Nebuchadnezzar, overwhelmed by the amazing greatness of the miracles, did not realize what he was doing, but coming to know the true God and Lord of kings he both worshipped His servant and offered him incense.

Verse 48. "Then the king elevated Daniel to a high position, and gave him many great gifts (A) and set him up as governor over all the provinces of Babylon. ... ." In this matter also the slanderous critic of the Church has ventured to castigate the prophet because he did not reject the gifts and because he willingly accepted honor of the Babylonians. He fails to consider the fact that it was for this very purpose that the king had beheld the dream and that the secrets of its interpretation were revealed by a mere lad, that Daniel might increase in importance and that in the place of captivity he might become ruler over all the Chaldeans, to the end that the omnipotence of God might be made known. We read that this same thing happened in the case of Joseph at the court of Pharaoh and in Egypt (Gen. 41), and also in the case of Mordecai at the court of Ahasuerus (Esth. 8). The purpose was that the Jews, as captives and (B) sojourners in each of these nations, might receive encouragement as they beheld men of their own nation constituted as governors over the Egyptians or the Chaldeans, as the case might be.

Verse 49. "Moreover Daniel made request of the king, and he appointed Shadrach, Meshach, and Abednego over the public works of the province of Babylon. But Daniel himself was in the king's gate." Daniel does not forget those men with whom he had made intercession to the Lord, and who had shared his peril with him. And so he makes them judges over the province, while he himself does not leave (a variant reading is: "did not leave") the king's side.

CHAPTER THREE
Verse 1. "Nebuchadnezzar the king made a golden statue seventy cubits in height and six cubits in breadth." How soon he forgot the truth, when he had just been worshipping a servant of God as if he had been God Himself, but now commanded a statue to be made for himself in order that he personally might be worshipped in the statue! Now if this statue was of gold (C), and was of incalculable weight, it was intended to arouse amazement in the beholders and to be worshipped as God even though a mere inanimate object, whilst everyone would be consecrating his own avarice to it. On the other hand an opportunity of salvation was afforded to the barbarian nations through the opportune presence of the captive Jews (Col. iii), with the result that after they had first come to know the power of the one true God through Daniel's revelation of the dream, they might then learn from the brave example of the three youths to despise death [variant: might learn that death ought to be despised], and to eschew the worship of idols.

"And he set it up in the plain of Dura in the province of Babylon." Instead of "Dura" Theodotion has "Deira," and Symmachus has (D) "Durau," whereas the Septuagint renders it as the common noun peribolon, a word which we might render as "game-preserve" or "enclosure."

Verse 2. "Nebuchadnezzar sent therefore to the satraps, magistrates and judges, the dukes and potentates, and the prefects and (E) all the princes of the various districts that they should gather themselves together." It is the higher ranks which stand in the greater peril, and those who occupy the loftier position are the more sudden in their fall. The princes are assembled to worship the statue in order that through their princes the nations also might be attracted into error, For those who possess riches and power are all the more easily overthrown because of their apprehension of being bereft of them. But after the magistrates are led astray, the subject populace perish through the evil example of their superiors.

Verses 4, 5. "And a herald proclaimed with mighty voice: 'To us the order is given, both peoples and tribes and languages, at what hour ye hear the sound of the trumpet. . ..'" Not that the entire population of all the nations could have gathered on the plain of Dura and adored the golden statue, but rather, in the person of their leaders, all the tribes and peoples were supposed to have performed the act of worship. Now as I mentally run through all the Holy Scripture, I nowhere find (unless my memory fails me) a passage stating that any of the saints worshipped God Himself by falling prostrate [actually there are many instances; cf. Brown-Driver-Briggs Hebrew Lexicon, 1005]; but only someone worshipping idols or demons or forbidden objects is said to have worshipped by falling prostrate. So also in this present instance that kind of worship is performed not once but several times as well. Moreover, in the Gospel the devil says to the Lord, "All these things will I give Thee, if Thou fallest down and worshippest me" (Matt. 4:9). But this comment should also be made, that all heretics who devise a false doctrine with the brilliance of worldly eloquence, fashion thereby a golden statue, and to the best of their ability constrain men by their persuasiveness to fall down and adore the idol of deceit.

Verse 7. "After these things the people, therefore, as soon as they heard the sound of the trumpet and pipe...." We are to take this statement in the same sense as above, so that we understand that all the peoples were represented by their leaders. For of course it was impossible for all the nations to attend at one time.

Verse 8. "And straightway at that time there came certain Chaldeans and accused the Jews...." They were envious of these Jews because they had been in charge of the king's business in Babylon, and also they were offended by their foreign religion and aversion towards idols. They therefore find a pretext for accusing them to the king. The final consequence ensues.

Verse 12. "Now then, there are certain Jews whom thou hast appointed over the affairs of the district of Babylon, namely Shadrach, Meshach, and Abednego, who have despised thy decree" (the Vulgate reads: "those men of thine have despised the decree, O king"). To a certain extent their statement amounts to this: "Those captives and slaves whom thou hast preferred before us and hast made to be governors have lifted themselves up in pride and despise thine orders, not serving thy gods, and not worshipping the golden statue thou hast set up." The assertion we made at the commencement of the commentary on the vision is more abundantly proved in this passage, namely that the gods of Nebuchadnezzar were not to be identified with the golden statue which he had ordered to be erected for the worship of himself, for in what follows the king himself says:

Verse 14. "Do ye not serve my gods, and do you not worship the golden statue which I have set up?. . ." Other authorities assert that it is the custom of Holy Scripture to speak of the one and same idol in the plural, just like the verse in Exodus concerning the calf: "These are thy gods, O Israel, who have brought thee out of the land of Egypt" (Ex. 22:4). Also in the Book of Kings, where Jeroboam is establishing the golden calf in Bethel, he is said to have fashioned idols (I Kings 12). On the other hand a plurality of demons are addressed in the singular number, as in Isaiah: "He bows himself down and worships it, and as he makes his vow he says, 'Thou art my God!'" (Isa. 44:17).

Verse 15. "Prostrate yourselves and worship the statue I have made." Although he had up to this point given the youths his orders in angry fashion, yet he gives them room for a change of heart, so that their previous guilt might be pardoned if only they should fall down and worship. But if they should not deign to offer worship, the punishment of the fiery furnace lay at hand.

"And what God is there who shall rescue you from my hand?..." Why naturally, that same God whose servant thou didst just recently worship and Whom thou didst assert to be truly God of gods and Lord of kings.

Verse 16. "King Nebuchadnezzar, we ought not to render thee answer concerning this matter." In the Hebrew [i.e., Chaldee] original there is no vocative "King" (A) as there is in the Septuagint, lest they should seem to address the ungodly man with servile flattery or to term him a king who was trying to force them to wickedness. But if it be contended that the reading, "O king!" should be included, then we may say that the youths were not impudently challenging the king to shed their blood but rendering him due honor so as to avoid injury to the true religion of God. But as for their statement. "We ought not to render thee answer concerning this matter," the meaning is: "Thou hast no need to hear words from men whose bravery and firmness thou wilt presently test by actual deeds."

Verse 17. "For behold, our God whom we serve is able to rescue us from the furnace of burning fire and to free us from thy hands, O king!" Where he had imagined he was frightening mere youths, he perceives in them a nature of manly courage. Nor do they speak of deliverance as delayed to the distant future, but rather they promise themselves immediate succor, asserting, "For behold, our God whom we serve is the One who is able to free us both from the fearsome flames thou threatenest and from thy hands."

Verse 18. "But if He does not will to do so"----a phrasing which admirably avoids the idea, "If He is not able," which would be inconsistent with what they had just asserted, "He is able to deliver us" ---- but rather they say, "If He does not will to do so." Thereby they indicate that it will not be a matter of God's inability but rather of His sovereign will if they do perish.

"Be it known to thee, O king, that we do not serve thy gods and do not worship the golden statue which thou hast set up." Whether we wish to read "statue" as Symmachus does, or "golden image" as the other authorities have rendered it, those who reverence God are not to worship it. Therefore, let judges and princes who worship the statues of emperors or idols realize that they are doing precisely the thing which the three youths refused to do and thereby pleased God. And we should observe the proper significance of the issue involved: they assert that worshipping the mere image is equivalent to serving the false gods themselves, neither of which things is befitting to the servants of God.

Verse 19. "Then Nebuchadnezzar was filled with rage, and (B) the aspect of his countenance was wholly altered." In certain Psalms the titles contain the notation; "On behalf of those who are to be wholly altered." [This is a literal rendering of the Septuagint's erroneous translation of the Hebrew title 'al shoshanni'm, which occurs in Psalm 45 and Psalm 69, and signifies: "Upon anemonies."] And so the expression "wholly altered" is ambiguous, comprising both the idea of change for the worse or change for the better. Now of course the alteration of Nebuchadnezzar's visage cannot be reconciled with a favorable sense. And after all there are some authorities who refer even the Psalm-titles to a change for the worse, on the ground that those who by nature have known God have been changed by the vexation and fury of their mind to a position of hostility towards Christ and His saints.

Verse 20. "And he gave orders that the furnace be fired to sevenfold intensity beyond its usual temperature, (C) and he commanded the strongest men in his army to bind the legs of Shadrach, Meshach and Abednego and cast them into the furnace of flaming fire." Just as if the usual fire without multiplied intensity could not have consumed the youths' bodies! But a fury and rage which borders on madness can observe no bounds. Also, he wished by the threat of intensified punishment to terrify those who seemed prepared for death.

Verse 21. "And straightway those men, bound up (D) in their trousers and turbans and footgear and garments, were cast into the midst of the furnace of flaming fire. ..." Instead of sarbal, "trousers" [actually this word probably meant "mantle" in the Aramaic] interpreted by Symmachus as anaxy-rides ("trousers"), Aquila and Theodotion read simply saraballa rather than the corrupt reading (E) sarabara. Now the shanks and shin-bones are called saraballa in the language of the Chaldeans [apparently erroneous information; the lexicons give only "trousers" or, preferably, "mantle"], and by extension of the same word it is applied to those articles of clothing which cover the shanks and shins, as if they were to be called "shankies" and "shinnies" (crurales et tibiales). "Turban," however, is a Greek word, tiara [actually the Aramaic is karbela, "cap"] which has by usage become a Latin word also, and Virgil says of it (Aeneid, VII):

"Both scepter and sacred tiara."

[Since tiara does not appear in the Aramaic original at all, the comment upon it seems quite misleading to a public not having access to the original. Two other comments ought to be made about Jerome's treatment of this verse: a) he puts "turbans" before "footgear" (pattish) instead of after it as the original does; b) he has nevertheless consulted the original carefully, since he avoids the variant reading of the LXX, which latter substitutes "upon their heads" for the word "footgear."] It was, however, a kind of skull-cap used by the Persian and Chaldean races.

Verse 22. "Then those same men who had cast Shadrach, Meshach, and Abednego were slain by the fiery flame." Of course this meant the same men of whom it was said above, "And he commanded the strongest men in his army to bind the legs of Shadrach, Meshach and Abednego and cast them into the burning furnace of fire (another reading: into the furnace of flaming fire)." And so they were not any chance servants of his whom Nebuchadnezzar destroyed, but men who of all his army were strong and most ready for war. Not only was it intended that the miracle should strike terror but also that his own army might experience injury.

Verse 23. "But these three men, (here the Vulgate inserts: "that is,") Shadrach, Meshach, and Abednego, fell fettered into the midst of the furnace of flaming fire. And they were walking about in the midst of the flames praising God and blessing the Lord. And Azariah stood and prayed after this fashion, opening his mouth in the midst of the fire and saying. . .." It was a great miracle for men to be cast into a furnace bound and to fall headlong into the midst of the fire, only to have the bonds burn up by which they were bound, the bodies of the fettered withal remaining untouched by the timid flames. The Hebrew text goes only up to this point and the intervening passage which now follows as far as the end of the Song of the Three Youths is not contained in the Hebrew [i.e. the Aramaic]. Lest we seem to pass over it altogether, we must make a few observations.

Verse 26. "Blessed art Thou, O Lord God of our fathers, and Thy name is to be praised and glorified forever, for Thou art just in all that Thou hast done to us" (the Vulgate adds: "in our case"). (A) Whenever we are oppressed by various anxieties, let us lovingly speak forth this sentiment with our whole heart, and whatever may have befallen us, let us confess that it is only right for us to endure it, that the scripture may be fulfilled in us: "The daughters of Judah have exulted and rejoiced in all Thy judgments, O Lord" (Ps. 96:8).

Verse 29. "For we have sinned and acted wickedly in departing from Thee, and we have forsaken Thee in all things." Now of course the three youths had not sinned, nor were they old enough when brought to Babylon to warrant being punished for their own faults. Consequently they were speaking as representatives of their people, in the same manner as the Apostle had to state: "For what I wish to do, that I do not; but what I do not want, that I carry into effect" (Rom 7:19), and so on with the rest of that same passage.

Verse 37. "Forasmuch, O Lord, as we have been diminished more than all the other races and abased in all the world this day because of our sins, and have at the present time neither prince nor prophet nor leader. . ." (B). These verses are to be used whenever the churches suffer want (because of the sins of the people) of holy men, and of magistrates who are most learned in the law of God, and also whenever in times of persecution no sacrifice or oblation is offered up. Some authorities relate this passage to the heavenly Jerusalem, on the ground that the souls have been plunged to the earthly plane and find themselves in a place of tears and utter distress, and bewail the sins of by-gone years and the other things included in the prophetic discourse. But the Church of God has not accepted this view.

Verse 39. "But in a contrite heart and humble spirit let us be accepted, like as in the burnt offerings of rams and bullocks...." (cf. Ps. 51:19). On the basis of the passage before us and also on the basis of what follows: "Bless the Lord, ye spirits and souls of the righteous," and also in view of the passage in Psalms: "The sacrifice for God is an anguished spirit, a contrite and abased heart God does not despise," certain authorities (C) would have it that there resides in man a spirit, distinct from the Holy Spirit and different from the soul itself. But they will have to work out the difficulty of how there can be said to be two substances and two inner selves in one and the same man, entirely apart from the body and from the grace of the Holy Spirit.

Verse 46. "And the king's servants who had cast them in did not cease to make the furnace hot with naphtha and pitch." Sallust (D) in his histories writes that naphtha is a kind of tinder in use among the Persians which furnishes the utmost encouragement to fires. Others are of the opinion that naphtha is the name applied to olive-pits which are thrown away when the dregs of the oil have dried up. In the same way, they assert, the Greek term pyrine is derived from its property of nourishing pyr, that is, "fire".

19

Verse 49. "But the angel of the Lord came down into the furnace with Azariah and his companions, and he smote the flame of the fire out of the furnace. ..." When the soul is oppressed with tribulation and taken up with various vexations, having lost hope of human aid and turned with its whole heart to God, an angel of the Lord descends to it. That is to say, the supernatural being descends to the aid of the servant and dashes aside the fierce heat of the violent flames, that the fiery shafts of the enemy utterly fail to pierce the inner citadel of our heart and we escape being shut up in his fiery furnace.

Verses 57, 58. "All ye works of the Lord, bless the Lord; laud Him and highly exalt Him forever. Praise Him, ye angels of the Lord; laud Him and highly exalt Him. ..." Having prefaced with general terms of praise, to the effect that every creature ought to praise the Lord, he addresses his exhortation in what follows to the various individual orders of creation: to the angels, the heavens, the waters and nature-forces, the sun and the moon, the rain-cloud and the dew, the wind, the fire and the billow, the cold and the heat, and all the rest too lengthy to include, so that he summons springs also and the seas, the sea-monsters and the birds, the beasts and flocks, to the praise of the Lord. He summons also the sons of men, and after the human race in general he specifies the race of Israel in particular, and of the Israelites themselves the priests and servants of the Lord, and the spirits and souls of the righteous, and those who are holy and of humble heart. And at the very last he specifies Hananiah, Azariah, and Mishael, who are summoned to praise the Lord for His present kindness. But all creation praises God not in word but indeed, inasmuch as the Creator is logically apprehended on the basis of His creatures, and in the various works and affections [unless affectibus be a misprint for effectibus: "operations"] the grandeur of God is made manifest.

Verse 87. "Bless Him, ye saints and humble of heart...." We are taught to have humbleness of heart both by this present verse and also by the statement in the Gospel: "Learn of Me, for I am meek and lowly in heart, and ye shall find rest for your souls" (Matt. 11:29). But this humbleness of heart is the same thing as is elsewhere called poverty in spirit, so that we are not to be lifted up in pride or seek after glory by a pretended humility, but rather that we abase ourselves with our whole heart. Up to this point we have mentioned but briefly a few things from Theodotion's edition, since the confession and the praises of the three youths are passages not contained in the Hebrew. But from this point on we shall follow the authentic Hebrew itself.

Verses 91, 92 (=24, 25). "Then Nebuchadnezzar the king was astounded and hastily arose and said to his nobles: 'Did we not cast three men in shackles into the midst of the fire?'" [When figures are given in parentheses they indicate the versification in the KJV.] After the princes have been punished, the king is rebuked, in order that he may glorify God while still alive. But he questions his nobles, by whose accusation and plot he had cast the three youths into the fiery furnace, so that when they reply that they had cast three youths into the furnace, he might announce and show forth to them (what had happened) (A).

"And they said to the king in reply, 'Truly, O king!' The king answered (the Vulgate omits "the king"): 'Behold, I see four men unbound and walking about in the midst of the fire, and they have no hurt, and the appearance of the fourth man (B) is the likeness of a son of God.' " Let me say again, how wise was the fire and how indescribable the power of God! Their bodies had been bound with chains; those chains were burnt up, whereas the bodies themselves were not burnt. As for the appearance of the fourth man, which he asserts to be like that of a son of God, either we must take him to be an angel, as the Septuagint has rendered it, or indeed, as the majority think, the Lord our Savior. Yet I do not know how an ungodly king could have merited a vision of the Son of God. On that reasoning one should follow Symmachus, who has thus interpreted it: "But the appearance of the fourth is like unto the sons," not unto the sons of God but unto gods themselves. We are to think of angels here, who after all are very frequently called gods as well as sons of God. So much for the story itself. But as for its typical significance, this angel or son of God foreshadows our Lord Jesus Christ, who descended into the furnace of hell, in which the souls of both sinners and of the righteous were imprisoned, in order that He might without suffering any scorching by fire or injury to His person deliver those who were held imprisoned by chains of death.

Verse 93 (=26). "Then Nebuchadnezzar approached unto the mouth of the burning fiery furnace and said: 'Shadrach, Meshach, and Abednego, servants of the Most High God, come forth and draw near!' And straightway Shadrach, Meshach, and Abednego came forth from the midst of the fire." Being terrified with fear, the king does not address his request to the youths through any messengers, but himself calls upon them by name, addressing them as servants of the Most High God, and begging these very men to come forth whom he himself had cast bound into the furnace.

Verse 95 (=28). " 'Blessed be God (the Vulgate has "their God, namely") of Shadrach, Meshach, and Abednego, Who hath sent His angel and rescued His servants who believed in Him. . ..' " The person whom he had previously called a son of God he here calls an angel, even though he had in the preceding passage described him as similar to a son of God rather than to God Himself. A second time, therefore, Nebuchadnezzar resumes a confession of faith in God, and as he condemns idols he praises the three youths who refused to serve or worship any god but their own God. Moreover he marvels that the fire was unable to affect the saints of God, for he says:

Verse 96 (=29). "'I have therefore determined upon this decree (the Vulgate says: "have appointed this decree"): that any people, tribe or tongue which utters blasphemy against the God of Shadrach, Meshach and Abednego shall utterly perish and his house shall be laid waste. For there is no other God who can save after such a fashion.' " Some authorities very wrongly apply this to the devil himself, asserting that in the consummation at the end of the world even the devil himself will receive a knowledge of God and will exhort all men to repent. These persons would have it that this is the king of Nineveh who finally descends from his proud throne and attains to the rewards of humility.

Verse 97 (=30). "Then the king promoted Shadrach, Meshach and Abednego to honor in the province of Babylon." Those commentators who say that the three youths were previously not judges set over the provinces but mere overseers of individual government agencies in Babylon, would have it that they were now appointed as judges over the provinces.

CHAPTER FOUR

Verse 98ff. (=1ff.) [The Hebrew Bible continues chap. III up through what is IV:3 in the English Bible] "Nebuchadnezzar the king unto all the peoples, nations and languages who dwell upon the whole earth: peace be multiplied unto you. The Most High God hath performed signs and wonders towards me. Therefore I have thought it well to declare His signs, for they are great, and His marvels, for they are mighty, and His kingdom, because it is (the Vulgate omits "because it is") an eternal kingdom, and His dominion is from generation to generation." The epistle of Nebuchadnezzar was inserted in the volume of the prophet, in order that the book might not afterwards be thought to have been manufactured by some other author, as the accuser (Porphyry) falsely asserts, but the product of Daniel himself.

Verse 1 (=4). "I, Nebuchadnezzar, was at ease in my house and prospering in my palace." The narrative is clear indeed and requires but little interpretation. Because he displeased God, Nebuchadnezzar was turned into a madman and dwelt for seven years amongst the brute beasts and was fed upon the roots of herbs. Afterwards by the mercy of God he was restored to his throne, and praised and glorified the King of heaven, on the ground that all His works are truth and His ways are justice and He is able to abase those who walk in pride. But there are some who claim to understand by the figure of Nebuchadnezzar the hostile power which the Lord speaks of in the Gospel, saying: "I beheld Satan falling from heaven like lightning" (Luke 10:18). Likewise John in Revelation, in the passage where the dragon falls upon the earth drawing a third of the stars with him (Rev. 12). Likewise Isaiah: "How hath the morning star fallen, which used to rise early in the morning" (Isa. 14:22). These authorities assert that it was absolutely impossible for a man who was reared in luxury to subsist on hay for seven years and to dwell among wild beasts for seven years without being at all mangled by them. Also they ask how the imperial authority could have been kept waiting for a mere madman, and how so mighty a kingdom could have gone without a king for so long a period. If, on the other hand, anyone had succeeded him on the throne, how foolish he would have to be thought to surrender an imperial authority which he had possessed for so long. Such a thing would be especially incredible since the historical records of the Chaldeans contain no such record, and since they recorded matters of far less import, it is impossible that they should have left things of major importance unmentioned. And so they pose all of these questions (A) and offer as their own reply the proposition that since the episode does not stand up as genuine history, the figure of Nebuchadnezzar represents the devil. To this position we make not the slightest concession; otherwise everything we read in Scripture may appear to be imperfect representations and mere fables. For once men have lost their reason, who would not perceive them to lead their existence like brutish animals in the open fields and forest regions? And to pass over all other considerations, since Greek and Roman history offer episodes far more incredible, such as Scylla and the Chimaera, the Hydra and the Centaurs, and the birds and wild beasts and flowers and trees, the stars and the stones into which men are related to have been transformed, what is so remarkable about the execution of such a divine judgment as this for the manifestation of God's power and the humbling of the pride of kings? Nebuchadnezzar says, " 'I was at ease in my house and prospering in my palace. . ..' " or as Theodo-tion renders it "upon my throne." Now those who follow the interpretation we are opposing understand by the devil's home this world of ours. Concerning the world Satan himself in the Gospel says to the Savior: "All these things have been given over to me" (Matt. 4:9). Likewise the Apostle says: "The world lieth in the Wicked One" (I John 5).

Verse 2 (=5). "'I beheld a dream which terrified me, and my thoughts while upon my bed.. . .'" Let our opponents answer what kind of a dream the hostile power [i.e., Satan] would have seen, unless perhaps everything he appears to possess in this world is a mere shadowy dream.

" 'And the visions of my head greatly disturbed me.' " Note how Nebuchadnezzar realized that his visions were not those of his eyes and heart, but rather of his head, because it was for the glory of God's future servants that these secrets were being revealed to him.

Verse 6 (=8). " 'Then at last my associate, Daniel, (B) whose name according to the name of my god is Belteshazzar, entered before my presence.'" With the exception of the Septuagint translators (who for some reason or other have omitted this whole passage [i.e., vv. 6-9]), the other three translators [Aquila, Symmachus, and Theodotion] have translated the word [i.e. 'oh°rdn, a dubious word generally rendered as "at last" by modern translations, but here probably to be construed as "another"] as "associate" (collega). Consequently by the judgment of the teachers of the Church, the Septuagint edition has been rejected in the case of this book, and it is the translation of Theodotion which is commonly read, since it agrees with the Hebrew as well as with the other translators (C). Wherefore also Origen asserts in the ninth book of the Stromata that he is discussing the text from this point on in the prophecy of Daniel, not as it appears in the Septuagint, which greatly differs from the Hebrew original, but rather as it appears in Theodotion's edition.

" '. . .(Daniel) who has within him the spirit of the holy gods; and I related the dream unto him....'" Corresponding to the rendering here given, "of the holy god," we read in Chaldee (in which Daniel was composed) the words elain cadisin ('-l-h-y-n q-d-y-sh-y-n) [vocalized this would be 'elahin qaddishin], which means "holy gods" and not "holy God," as Theodotion rendered it. Nor is it surprising if Nebuchadnezzar made such a mistake, and supposed that any force he perceived to be higher than himself were gods, rather than God. Lastly, he states also in his following words: " 'Belteshazzar, thou chief of the soothsayers, whom I know to possess within thee the spirit of the holy gods.' " Belteshazzar was chief of the soothsayers or enchanters, as others have rendered it. It is not surprising if he had been appointed chief over all the soothsayers since he had at the king's order been taught the wisdom of the Chaldeans, and had besides been found ten times wiser than all the rest. Let us ask of those who do not concede any historical basis for this vision, what Nebuchadnezzar it was who saw the dream, and who the Daniel was who declared his dream and foretold things to come. And how did it come to pass that this same Daniel (whose fortitude was, at least according to them, to be understood as divine in origin) was appointed chief of the soothsayers by Nebuchadnezzar, and called his companion?

Verse 7 (=10). "'I saw, and behold there was a tree in the midst of the earth, and its height was very great. ...' " It was not only of Nebuchadnezzar, King of the Chaldeans, but also of all impious men that the prophet says: "I beheld the impious man highly exalted and lifted up like the cedars of Lebanon" (Ps. 36:35). [This is Ps. 37:35 in the English Bible, and preserves a different reading, taken over from the Septuagint, rather than the Hebrew reading: "... and spreading himself like a green tree in its native soil."] Such men are lifted up, not by the greatness of their virtues, but by their own pride; and for that reason they are cut down and fall into ruin. Therefore it is good to follow the teaching of our Lord in the Gospel: "Learn of Me, for I am meek and lowly in heart" (Matt. 11:29). But as for the fact that, according to Theodotion, he mentions his kutos or height ---- or else his kureia (A), as he himself later renders it, that is to say, his dominion (a word we have translated as "his appearance") ---- those same detractors of the historicity of this passage slanderously assert that Nebuchadnezzar's dominion never possessed the entire world. He did not rule over the Greeks or barbarians, or over all of the nations in the north and west, but only over the provinces of the East; that is to say, over Asia, not over Europe or Libya. Consequently all these slanders require to be understood as attributable to the devil, for actually we ourselves should accept all this as spoken by way of hyperbole, having in view the arrogance of the impious king, who in Isaiah (chap. 14) makes as great a boast as this, claiming that he possesses the very heaven itself, and the whole earth besides, as if it were a nest full of birds' eggs.

Verses 10, 11 (=13, 14). "'And behold, a watchman and a holy one descended from heaven, and he cried out with a loud voice and spoke as follows: 'Cut down the tree and chop off its branches.. . .'" Instead of "watchman" Theodotion uses the Chaldee word itself, hir, which is written with the three letters 'ayin, yodh, and resh. But it signifies the angels, because they ever keep watch and are prepared to carry out God's command. And so we too follow the example of the angels in their duties when we engage in frequent night-long vigils. Also it is said of the Lord: "He who keepeth Israel will neither slumber nor sleep" (Ps. 120:4, i.e. Ps. 121:4). Lastly, we read a little later: "In the decision of the watchmen, i.e., the angels, lies the decree and the speech and the petition of the holy ones." Moreover it is both Greek and (B) Latin usage to call the rainbow iris, because it is said to descend to earth in a multicolored arch.

Verse 16 (=19). "Then Daniel, whose name was Belteshazzar, began quietly to meditate by himself for about an hour, and his meditations greatly troubled him. And the king answered and said, 'Belteshazzar, let not the dream or its interpretation disturb you.' Belteshazzar answered and said...." Daniel silently understood that the dream was directed against the king, and the pallor of his countenance showed forth the fear in his heart, and he felt sorry for the man who had conferred upon him the greatest of honor. And to avoid all appearance of taunting the king or glorying over him as an enemy, he only told him what he understood of the matter after he had begged to be excused.

" 'My lord, (C) may this dream apply to those who hate thee, and its interpretation to thy foes.'" And so Nebuchadnezzar, seeing that Daniel was afraid of appearing to speak something of ill omen and against the king's interest, urged him to speak out plainly and truly what he understood of the matter without any apprehension.

Verse 17 (=20). " 'The lofty and vigorous tree which thou sawest, the height of which reached the heavens. .. .' " He explains the truth without insulting the king, so as to avoid appearing to charge the king with sinful pride, but rather with overweening greatness.

Verse 20 (=23). " 'Let him be bound with iron and with brass in the grass out of doors, and let him be sprinkled with dew of heaven, and let his feeding be with the wild beasts, until seven times pass over him.'" It was also written to the same effect above. And so those who object to the historicity of the narrative ask us how Nebuchadnezzar would have been bound with chains of iron and brass, or who would have bound him or tied him up with fetters. Yet it is very clear that all maniacs are bound with chains to keep them from destroying themselves or attacking others with weapons.

Verses 21, 22 (=24, 25). " 'This is the interpretation of the sentence of the Most High which has come upon my lord the king. They shall cast thee forth from among men and thy habitation shall be with cattle and wild beasts.. . .'" Daniel moderates the severity of the sentence by complimentary language, so that (variant: and) after he has first set forth the harsher aspects, he may moderate the king's alarm by assurances of the kindlier treatment to follow. He draws the final inference:

Verse 23 (=26). " 'Thy kingdom shall remain unto thee, after thou shalt have acknowledged that power belongs to Heaven.'" Those who contest the historicity of this incident and would have it that the devil's original position of honor will be restored to him, make capital of this passage, on the ground that after Nebuchadnezzar has during the seven-year cycle endured torments and bestialization, feeding upon grass and hay, he makes a confession of the Lord and becomes the person he was before. But they are bound to answer the question how it can be consistent for the angels who have never fallen to have someone rule over them once more who has only through repentance been restored to favor.

Verse 24 (=27). " 'Wherefore, O king, let my counsel meet with thy favor, and make up for thy sins by deeds of charity, and thine iniquities by showing mercy to the poor. Perhaps God will forgive thy transgressions.'" Since he had previously pronounced the sentence of God, which of course cannot be altered, how could he exhort the king to deeds of charity and acts of mercy towards the poor? This difficulty is easily solved by reference to the example of King Hezekiah, who Isaiah had said was going to die; and again, to the example of the Ninevites, to whom it was said: "Yet forty days, and Nineveh shall be destroyed" (Jonah 3). And yet the sentence of God was changed in response to the prayers of Hezekiah and the city of Nineveh, not by any means because of the ineffectualness of the judgment itself but because of the conversion of those who merited pardon. Morever in Jeremiah God states that He threatens evil for the nation (Jer. 23), but if it does that which is good, He will alter His threats to bestow mercy. Again, He affirms that He directs His promises to the man who does good; and if the same man thereafter works evil, He says that He changes His decision, not with regard to the men themselves, but with regard to their works which have thus changed in character. For after all, God is not angered at men but at their sins; and when no sins inhere in a man, God by no means inflicts a punishment which has been commuted. In other words, let us say that Nebuchadnezzar performed deeds of mercy toward the poor in accordance with Daniel's advice, and for that reason the sentence against him was delayed of execution for twelve months. But because he afterwards while walking about in his palace at Babylon said boastingly: "Is this not the great Babylon (A) which I myself have built up as a home for the king by the might of my power and the glory of my name?" therefore he lost the virtue of his charitableness by reason of the wickedness of his pride.

"It may be that God will forgive thy sins." In view of the fact that the blessed Daniel, foreknowing the future as he did, had doubts concerning God's decision, it is very rash on the part of those who boldly promise pardon to sinners. And yet it should be recognized that indulgence was promised to Nebuchadnezzar in return, as long as he wrought good works. Much more, then, is it promised to other men who have committed less grievous sins than he. We read in Jeremiah also of God's direction to the people of the Jews, that they should pray for the Babylonians, inasmuch as the peace of the captives was bound up with the peace of the captors themselves.

Verses 28, 29 (=31, 32). "While the saying was yet in the king's mouth, a voice from heaven assailed him: 'King Nebuchadnezzar, to thee it is spoken, thy kingdom shall pass away (variant reading: is passing away) from thee and they shall cast thee forth from among mankind.'" His arrogant boasting is immediately punished by the Lord. For this reason the execution of the sentence is not delayed, lest mercy towards the poor seem to have profited him not at all. But as soon as he has spoken in pride, he straightway loses the kingdom which had been reserved for him on account of his works of charity.

"...until thou dost recognize that the Most High reigns in the kingdom of men." In misery it comes as a great consolation to know, when one is in a painful situation, that a more favorable future will ensue. Yet Nebuchadnezzar's fury and madness were so pronounced that in time of affliction he would not have remembered the blessings which God had promised him.

Verse 31 (=34). " 'I, Nebuchadnezzar, lifted mine eyes toward heaven, and my intelligence returned to me.' " Had he not raised his eyes towards heaven, he would not have regained his former intelligence. Moreover, when he says that his intelligence returned to him, he shows that he had lost not his outward appearance but only his mind.

"'And His kingdom is from generation to generation.' " If we accept this expression in the Scriptures, "From generation to generation," as simply for what it is, then it unquestionably means "for all time to come." But if, on the other hand, "generation and generation" signifies (as we have often asserted) two generations, that of the Law and that of the Gospel, the question comes up as to how Nebuchadnezzar would have known of the unrevealed secrets ("sacraments") of God. [The original for "from generation to generation" is " 'im dar wedar," i.e., "with generation and generation," which Jerome renders as "in generatione et generatione" or "in generation and generation." Undoubtedly the idea of the original is distributive or successive: "unto each successive generation." Jerome's explanation of this characteristic Semitic phrase as an occult reference to the two dispensations of the Old and New Testaments seems very farfetched.] But perhaps we might say this, that after he raised his eyes towards heaven and received back his former estate and exalted and blessed the ever-living God, he would not have failed to know this secret also.

Verse 32 (=35). " 'For He does according to His will, just as (B) among the powers of heaven, so also among the inhabitants of the earth. ...' "This too Nebuchadnezzar expresses like a worldling. For God does not simply do what He wishes, but rather God wishes only that which is good. Nebuchadnezzar, however, expressed himself in this way, in order that even while he declared God's power, he might appear to impugn God's justice, on the ground that he had suffered unmerited punishment.

Verse 33 (=36). "'And my nobles and officers sought me out and I was restored to my kingdom, and all the greater magnificence accrued to me.' " Well then, according to those who argue against the historical character of this account, all the angelic powers are going to seek out the devil again, and he will increase to such a degree of might, that the very one who formerly exalted himself against God is going to be greater than he was before his sin.

Verse 34 (=37). " 'Now therefore 1, Nebuchadnezzar, do praise, magnify and glorify the King of heaven, for all His works are true and His ways are judgment, and He is able to humble those who walk in pride.' " Nebuchadnezzar understood the reason why he had suffered in seven years' punishment, and for that reason he humbled himself, since he had exalted himself against God.

CHAPTER FIVE
Verse 1. "Belshazzar the king made a great feast for his one thousand nobles; and each one drank in the order of his age." It should be known that this man was not the son of Nebuchadnezzar, as readers commonly imagine; but according to (C) Berosus, who wrote the history of the Chaldeans, and also Josephus, who follows Berosus, after Nebuchadnezzar's reign of forty-three years, a son named Evilmerodach succeeded to his throne. It was concerning this king that Jeremiah wrote that in the first year of his reign he raised the head of Jehoiachin, king of Judah, and took him out of his prison (Jer. 52). Josephus likewise reports that after the death of Evilmerodach, his son [actually his brother-in-law] Neriglissar succeeded to his father's throne; after whom in turn came his son (D) Labosordach, [the cuneiform spelling is Labashi-Marduk]. Upon the latter's death, his son, Belshazzar [note that Jerome is not aware of Belshazzar's father, Nabonidus], obtained the kingdom, and it is of him that the Scripture now makes mention. After he had been killed by Darius, King of the Medes, who was the maternal uncle of Cyrus, King of the Persians, the empire of the Chaldeans was destroyed by Cyrus the Persian. It was these two kingdoms [the Median and the Persian] which Isaiah in chap. 21 addresses as a charioteer of a vehicle drawn by a camel and an ass. Indeed,

Xenophon also writes the same thing in connection with the childhood of Cyrus the Great; likewise Pompeius Trogus and many others who have written up the history of the barbarians. Some authorities think that this Darius was the Astyages mentioned in the Greek writings, while others think it was Astyages' son, and that he was called by the other name among the barbarians. "And each one of the princes who had been invited drank in the order of his own age." Or else, as other translators have rendered it: "The king himself was drinking in the presence of all the princes whom he had invited." [The latter rendering seems to be the only one justified by the Aramaic original.]

Verse 2. "Being now drunken, he therefore gave order that the golden and silver vessels be brought in which his father, Nebuchadnezzar, had taken away from the temple which was in Jerusalem, in order that the king might drink from them. ..." The Hebrews hand down some such story as this: that up until the seventieth year, on which Jeremiah had said that the captivity of the Jewish people would be released (a matter of which Zechariah also speaks in the first part of his book), Belshazzar had esteemed God's promise to be of none effect; therefore he turned the failure of the promise into an occasion of joy and arranged a great banquet, scoffing somewhat at the expectation of the Jews and at the vessels of the Temple of God. Punishment, however, immediately ensued. And as to the fact that the author calls Nebuchadnezzar the father of Belshazzar, he does not make any mistake in the eyes of those who are acquainted with the Holy Scripture's manner of speaking, for in the Scripture all progenitors and ancestors are called fathers. This factor also should be borne in mind, that he was not sober when he did these things, but rather when he was intoxicated and forgetful of the punishment which had come upon his progenitor, Nebuchadnezzar.

Verse 4. "They were drinking wine and praising their gods of gold, of silver, of bronze, of iron, of wood, and of stone." How great was their folly! As they drank from golden vessels, they were praising gods of wood and of stone. As long as the vessels had been in the idol-temple of Babylon, God was not moved to wrath, for they had evidently consecrated the property of God to divine worship, even though they did so in accordance with their own depraved views of religion. But after they defiled holy things for the use of men, their punishment followed upon the heels of their sacrilege. Moreover, they were praising their own gods and scoffing at the God of the Jews, on the ground that they were drinking from His vessels because of the victory their own gods had bestowed upon them. Applying this figuratively, we should have to say that it applies to all the heretics or to any doctrine which is contrary to truth but which appropriates the words of the Biblical prophets and misuses the testimony of Scripture to suit its own inclination. It furnishes liquor to those whom it deceives and with whom it has committed fornication. It carries off the vessels of God's Temple and waxes drunker by quaffing them; and it does not give the praise to the God whose vessels they are, but to gods of gold and silver, of bronze, of iron, of wood, and of stone. I think that the golden ones (A) are those which consist of earthly reason. The silver gods are those which possess the charm of eloquence and are fashioned by rhetoric. But those which bring in the fables of the poets and employ ancient traditions containing marked divergences from one another in respect to good taste or folly, such are described as bronze and iron. And those who set forth sheer absurdities are called wooden or stone. The Book of Deuteronomy divides these all into two classes, saying: "Cursed is the man who fashions a graven image and a molten image, the work of the hands of an artificer, and sets it up in a secret place" (Deut. 32:15). For all heretics operate secretly and disguise their fallacious teachings, in order that they may from concealment shoot their arrows against those who are upright in heart.

Verse 5. "At that same hour some fingers appeared as if they were of a human hand, writing something over against the lampstand upon the surface of the wall of the king's palace. And the king watched the joints of the hand as it wrote." He puts it nicely when he says, "At that same hour," just as we earlier read concerning Nebuchadnezzar, "While the saying was yet in the king's mouth." This was in order that the offender might recognize that his punishment was not inflicted upon him for any other reason but his blasphemy.

But as for the circumstance that the fingers seemed to be writing on the wall over against the lampstand, this was to avoid having the hand and the written matter appear at too great a distance from the light (to be clearly visible). And the fingers wrote upon the wall of the royal palace in order that the king might understand that the inscription concerned himself.

Verse 6. "Then the king's expression was altered. ..." Here too it is to be observed concerning those Psalms entitled: "For those who will suffer alterations (or vicissitudes)," that the alteration of fortune is not only the lot of the saint but also of the sinner. ["For those who will suffer alteration" is a remarkable interpretation of the Hebrew (al-shoshannim)----"according to lilies" (RSV)----rendered in the Authorized Version as "upon Shoshannim." The Vulgate rendering, following that of the Septuagint, is based upon a very implausible vowel pointing: 'al-sheshonim.'] For we read in this connection: "King Belshazzar was considerably disturbed and his countenance was altered."

Verse 7. The king therefore cried out vehemently that the magicians should be brought in, and the Chaldeans and the soothsayers...." Forgetting about the experiences of Nebuchadnezzar, he was following after the ancient and ingrained error of his family, so that instead of summoning a prophet of God he summons the magicians and Chaldeans and soothsayers.

". . .he shall be clothed in purple and he shall have a golden necklace about his neck." It is, of course, ridiculous of me to argue about matters of gender in a commentary on the prophets; but inasmuch as an ignorant but ostentatious critic has rebuked me for changing "necklace" (torquis) from feminine to masculine, I will make the brief observation that while Cicero (B) and Vergil use "necklace" in the feminine, Livy uses it in the masculine.

"...and he shall be the third man in my kingdom. ..." That means either that he is to be third in rank after the king, or else one of the three princes of the realm----for we elsewhere read of the tristatai. [A tristates is one who stands next in rank to the king and queen, i.e., a vizier.]

Verse 10. "Now the queen, by reason of what had happened to the king and his nobles, entered into the banquet-hall. ..." Josephus says she was Belshazzar's grandmother, whereas Origen says she was his mother. She therefore knew about previous events of which the king was ignorant. So much for Porphyry's far-fetched objection [lit.: "Therefore let Porphyry stay awake nights"----evigilet], who fancies that she was the king's wife, and makes fun of the fact that she knows more than her husband does.

Verse 10 (=11). "'There is a man in thy kingdom who possesses within him the spirit of the holy gods.'" All the authorities except Symmachus, who adheres to the Chaldee original, render: "the spirit of God."

"'. .. and in the days of thy father, wisdom, and knowledge were found in him.. . .'" She calls Nebuchadnezzar his father, according to the custom of the Scriptures, even though, as we remarked before, he was actually his great-grandfather. But Daniel's godly manner of life even amongst the barbarians is worthy of our imitation, for the very grandmother or mother of the king extolled him with such words of praise because of the greatness of his virtues.

Verse 11 (sic!) (=17). "To this Daniel made answer before the king, saying: 'Thy gifts be unto thyself, and bestow the presents of thy house upon someone else. .. .'" We should follow the example of a man like Daniel, who despised the honor and gifts of a king, and who without any reward even in that early day followed the Gospel injunction: "Freely have ye received, freely give." And besides, when one is announcing sad tidings, it is unbecoming for him willingly to accept gifts.

Verse 19. "'He slew whomever he would and smote to death whomever he wished to; those whom he wished he set on high, and brought low whomever he would.'" Thus he sets forth the example of the king's great-grandfather, in order to teach him the justice of God and make it clear that his great-grandson too was to suffer similar treatment because of his pride. Now if Nebuchadnezzar slew whomever he would and smote to death whomever he wished to; if he set on high those whom he would and brought low whomever he wished to, there is certainly no Divine providence or Scriptural injunction behind these honors and slayings, these acts of promotion and humiliation. But rather, such things ensue from the will [reading voluntate for the erroneous voluntas of the text] of the men themselves who do the slaying and promoting to honor, and all the rest. If this be the case, the question arises as to how we are to understand the Scripture: "The heart of a king reposes in the hand of God; He will incline it in whatever direction He wishes" (Prov. 21:1). Perhaps we might say that every saint is a king, for sin does not reign in his mortal body, and his heart therefore is kept safe, for he is in God's hand (Rom. 6). And whatever has once come into the hand of God the Father, according to the Gospel, no man is able to take it away. And whoever is taken away, it is understood that he never was in God's hand at all.

Verses 22, 23. "'Thou too, his son, O Belshazzar, hast not humbled thine heart, even though thou knewest all these things, but hast lifted thyself up against the ruler of heaven....'" Because thy great-grandfather, she says, lifted up his heart and hardened his spirit in pride, he therefore was put down from his royal throne and his glory was taken away, and so on (Jer. 4) Therefore in thy case also, because thou knewest these things about thy relative and didst understand that God resists the proud and gives grace to the humble, thou shouldest not have lifted up thy heart against the ruler of heaven and scoffed at His majesty and perpetrated the deeds which thou hast. Some authorities apply this passage to Antichrist, on the ground that he has imitated the pride of his father, the Devil, and has raised himself up against God. But they must deal with the question of whom Daniel represents, and who is to be understood as interpreting the inscription of God, and who these Medes and Persians are who put Antichrist to death and succeed to his royal power. For there is no doubt but what it is the saints who are to rule after the Antichrist.

Verses 25-28. "This is the inscription which has been set up: MANE, THECEL, PHARES. And this is the interpretation of the sentence: 'MANE' means that God has numbered thy kingdom and brought it to an end. 'THECEL' means it has been weighed in the scales and has been found deficient (Vulg.: thou hast been weighed and hast been found. .. .). 'PHARES' means that thy kingdom has been removed and given to the Medes and Persians." The inscription (A) of these three words on the wall simply meant: "Mane, Thecel, Phares"; the first of which sounds forth the idea of "number," and the second "a weighing out," and the third "removal." And so there was a need not only for reading the inscription but also for interpreting what had been read, in order that it might be understood what these words were announcing. That is to say, that God had numbered his kingdom and brought it to an end, and that He had seized hold upon him to weigh him in His judgment-scales, and the sword would slay him before he should meet a natural death; and that his empire would be divided among the Medes and Persians. For Cyrus, the king of the Persians, as we have already mentioned, overthrew the Chaldean Empire in alliance with Darius, his maternal uncle.

Verse 29. "Then at the kings order Daniel was clothed with purple and a golden chain was placed around his neck, and he was proclaimed to have authority as third ruler in the kingdom." Or else, it might be construed as having authority over a third part of the kingdom. At any rate he received the royal insignia of necklace and purple, with the result that he appeared more notable to Darius, who was to be the successor in the royal power, and all the more honorable because of his notability. Nor was it strange that Belshazzar should have paid the promised reward upon hearing sad tidings. For either he supposed that his predictions would take place in the distant future, or else he hoped he would obtain mercy by honoring the prophet of God. And if he did not obtain this boon, it was because his sacrilege toward God outweighed the honor he accorded to man.

Verses 30, 31. "On that same night Belshazzar, King of the Chaldeans, was slain, and Darius the Mede succeeded to his kingdom at the age of sixty-two." Josephus writes in his tenth book of the Jewish Antiquities that when Babylon had been laid under siege by the Medes and Persians, that is, by Darius and Cyrus, Belshazzar, King of Babylon, fell into such forgetfulness of his own situation as to put on his celebrated banquet and drink from the vessels of the Temple, and even while he was besieged he found leisure for banqueting. From this circumstance the historical account could arise, that he was captured and slaughtered on the same night, while everyone was either terrified by fear of the vision and its interpretation, or else taken up with festivity and drunken banqueting. As for the fact that while Cyrus, King of the Persians, was the victor, and Darius was only King of the Medes, it was Darius who was recorded to have succeeded to the throne of Babylon, this was an arrangement occasioned by factors of age, family relationship, and the territory ruled over. By this I mean that Darius was sixty-two years old, and that, according to what we read, the kingdom of the Medes was more sizable than that of the Persians, and being Cyrus's uncle, he naturally had a prior claim, and ought to have been accounted as successor to the rule of Babylon. Therefore, also in a vision of Isaiah which was recited against Babylon, after many other matters too lengthy to mention, an account is given of these things which are to take place: "Behold I Myself will rouse up against them the Medes, a people who do not seek after silver nor desire gold, but who slay the very children with their arrows and have no compassion upon women who suckle their young" (B) (Isa. 13:7). And Jeremiah says: "Sanctify nations against her, even the kings of Media, and the governors thereof and all the magistrates thereof and all the land under the power thereof" (Jer. 51:28). Then follow the words: "The daughter of Babylon is like a threshing-floor during the time of its treading; yet a little while, and the time of its harvesting will come" (Jer. 51:33). And in testimony of the fact that Babylon was captured during a banquet, Isaiah clearly exhorts her to battle when he writes: "Babylon, my beloved, has become a strange spectacle unto me [this rendering differs from the Hebrew original and the Septuagint, and seems altogether unjustified]: set thou the table and behold in the mirrors [the Hebrew says: "set the watch"] those who eat and drink; rise up, ye princes, and snatch up your shields!" (Isa. 21:4, 5).

CHAPTER SIX
Verses 1 ff. "It pleased Darius to appoint over his kingdom one hundred and twenty satraps, that they might be throughout his whole kingdom; and over them there were three princes, of which Daniel was one." Josephus, of whom we made mention above, in writing an account of this passage, put it this way: Now Darius (C), who destroyed the empire of the Babylonians in cooperation with his relative, Cyrus, ---- for they carried on the war as allies ---- was sixty-two years of age at the time he captured Babylon. He was the son of Astyages, and was known to the Greeks by another name. Moreover he took away the prophet Daniel with him and took him to Media, and made him one of the three princes who were in charge of his whole kingdom. Hence we see that when Babylon was overthrown, Darius returned to his own kingdom in Media, and brought Daniel along with him in the same honorable capacity to which he had been promoted by Belshazzar. There is no doubt but what Darius had heard of the sign and portent which had come to Belshazzar, and also of the interpretation which

Daniel had set forth, and how he had foretold the rule of the Medes and the Persians. And so no one should be troubled by the fact that Daniel is said in one place to have lived in Darius's reign, and in another place in the reign of Cyrus. The Septuagint rendered Darius by the name Artaxerxes. But as for the fact that a non-chronological order is followed, so that some history is narrated in the reign of Darius before material is given for Belshazzar's reign [cf. 7:1 and 8:1, which of course follow chap. 6], whereas we are subsequently to read that he was put to death by Darius, it seems to me that the anachronism results from the fact that the author has brought all the historical portions together in immediate sequence. Therefore it is at the close of the earlier vision that he had stated: "And Darius the Mede succeeded to the realm at the age of sixty-two." And so it was under this Darius who put Belshazzar to death that the events took place of which we are about to speak.

"Moreover the king was planning to set Daniel over the whole realm. Consequently the princes and satraps sought an opportunity to find out something against Daniel as touching the king...." Instead of "princes" ----the rendering used by Symmachus ---- Theodotion translated it as taktikoi ["military tacticians"], and Aquila as synektikoi ["liaison officers?"]. And when I inquired as to who these tacticians or liaison princes might be, I read it more clearly specified in the Septuagint, which renders: "...and the two men whom the king had appointed with Daniel, and also the one hundred twenty satraps." And so it was the fact that the king was planning to appoint Daniel as chief ruler even over the two princes who had been associated with him in a triumvirate that gave rise to the envy and intrigue. (A) They sought an opportunity to find out something against Daniel as touching the king [literally: "from the side of the king," representing the Aramaic "missad malkuta'" ----"from the side of the kingdom"]. And in this passage the Jews have ventured some such deduction as this: the side of the king is tantamount to the queen or his concubines and other wives who slept at his side. And so they were seeking for a pretext in things of this sort, to see whether they could accuse Daniel of wrong in his speech or touch or movements of his head or any of his sensory organs. But, say the Jews, they could find no cause for suspicion whatsoever. Since he was a eunuch, they could not even accuse him on the score of lewdness. This interpretation was made by those [Jews], who make a practice of fabricating long tales on the pretext of a single word. I myself would simply interpret this as meaning that they were unable to discover any pretext of accusation against him in any matter in which he had injured the king, for the simple reason that he was a faithful man and no suspicion of blame was discoverable in him. Instead of "suspicion" Theodotion and Aquila have rendered "offense" (amblakema), which is essaitha in the Chaldee (B). And when I asked a Jew for the meaning of this word, he replied that the basic significance of it was "snare," and we may render it as a "lure" or sphalma, that is, a "mistake." Furthermore Euripides in his "Medea" equates the word amplakiai ["offenses"] (spelling it with a p instead of a b) to hamartiai, that is to say, "sins."

Verse 5. "Therefore those men said: 'We will not find any pretext against Daniel, except perhaps in the law of his God.'" Blessed indeed is a life so led that even enemies can find no cause for accusation, except perhaps in matter pertaining to God's law.

Verse 6. "Then the princes and satraps privily withdrew to the king and thus spoke to him." It was well said that they privily withdrew [or "went surreptitiously"] for they did not come right out with what they were aiming at, but contrived their plot against a private enemy on the pretext of honoring the king.

Verse 8. "Now therefore, O king, confirm the measure and write the decree so that it may not be altered, according to the custom established by the Medes and Persians." It is perfectly evident, as we have remarked above, that there was only one kingdom of the Medes and Persians both, under the rule of Darius and Cyrus.

Verse 10. "Now when Daniel learned of it, that is, of the law which had been enacted, he entered his house, and with the windows in his upper room opened up in the direction of Jerusalem, he continued to bow his knees three times a day and worshipped, and made confession before his God just as he was previously accustomed to do." We must quickly draw from our memory and bring together from all of Holy Scripture all the passages where we have read of domata, which mean in Latin either "walled enclosures" (menia) (C) or "beds" or "sun-terraces," and also the references to anogaia (D), that is, "upper rooms." For after all, our Lord celebrated the passover in an upper room (Matt. 14), and in the Acts of the Apostles the Holy Spirit came upon the one hundred and twenty souls of believers while they were in an upper room (Acts 2). And so Daniel in this case, despising the king's commands and reposing his confidence in God, does not offer his prayers in some obscure spot, but in a lofty place, and opens up his windows towards Jerusalem, from whence he looked for the peace [of God]. He prays, moreover, according to God's behest, and also according to what Solomon had said when he admonished the people that they should pray in the direction of the Temple. Furthermore, there are three times in the day when we should bow our knees unto God, and the tradition of the Church understands them to be the third hour, the sixth hour, and the ninth hour [i.e., 9:00 A.M., 12:00 M., and 3:00 P.M.]. Lastly, it was at the third hour that the Holy Spirit descended upon the Apostles (Acts 3) [misprint for Acts 2:15]. It was at the sixth hour that Peter, purposing to eat, ascended to the upper room for prayer (Acts 10). It was at the ninth hour that Peter and John were on their way to the Temple (Acts 3).

Verse 11. "Those men, therefore, conducted an inquisitive search and discovered Daniel in prayer and making supplication unto his God." From this passage we learn that we are not to expose ourselves rashly to danger, but so far as it lies in our power, we are to avoid the plots of our enemies. And so in Daniel's case, he did not contravene the king's authority in a public square or out in the street, but rather in a private place, in order that he might not neglect the commands of the one true God Almighty.

Verse 12. " 'Hast thou not ordained, O king, that any man who makes a request of any other person besides thee, whether god or man, shall be thrown into the lion-pit?' The king answered them, saying. ..." They do not mention Daniel's name, so that when the king has made a general answer as to the order he gave, he may then be bound by his own word, and not deal with Daniel in any other fashion than he has stated.

" 'What you have said is true, according to the decree of the Medes and Persians, which it is not lawful to violate.' " We repeatedly take note of every passage which speaks of the kingdom of the Medes and Persians, so that we may dispose of the knotty problem of why Daniel speaks of the kingdom in one place as being under Darius, and in another as being under Cyrus.

Verse 13. "Then they answered before the king and said, 'Daniel, who is of the captivity of Judah, has paid no heed to thy law....'" In order to magnify (A) the dishonor involved in this contempt, they speak of the man who showed this contempt for the king's commands as a mere captive.

Verse 14. "And when the king heard this statement, he became quite grieved and applied himself on Daniel's behalf that he might deliver him." He realized that he had been tripped up by his own reply to their question, and also that envy was the motive of their plot. And so to avoid the appearance of acting against his own law, he wanted to deliver Daniel from danger by ingenuity and strategy rather than by exerting his royal authority. And so earnestly did he labor and strive that he would not accept any food, absolute monarch though he was, even until sunset. And as for the plotters, so firmly did they persist in their evil purpose that no consideration of the king's personal desire or of the damage he would sustain had any effect upon them.

Verse 15. "But those men, understanding the king's intent, said to him: 'Be it known to thee, O king, that no law of the Medes and Persians, nor any decree which the king has enacted, is capable of alteration.' " Just as the king understood that the princes were making their accusation out of motives of envy, so also they for their part understood what the king's purpose was, namely that he wished to rescue Daniel from imminent death. And so they allege that according to the law of the Medes and Persians, the commands of a king cannot be nullified.

Verse 16. "Then the king gave order, and they brought Daniel and cast him into the pit of lions. And the king said to Daniel: 'Thy God whom thou dost ever serve will Himself deliver thee.'" He gives way to the crowd and dares not to withhold from his plotting adversaries the death of his friend, and he commits to the power of God the purpose which he himself was unable to attain. Nor does he use the language of doubt, so as to say, "If He be able to deliver thee"; but rather he speaks with boldness and confidence and says, "The God whom thou dost ever serve shall Himself deliver thee." He had heard, of course, that three youths who were of a lower rank than Daniel himself had triumphed over the flames of Babylon. He had heard that many secrets had been revealed to Daniel, and therefore regarded him highly, and held him, captive though he was, in the greatest honor.

Verse 17. "A single stone was brought and placed over the opening of the pit, and the king sealed it with his ring... ." He sealed with his ring the rock by which the opening of the pit was shut up, so that the enemies of Daniel might not make any attempt to harm him. For he had entrusted him to the power of God, and although not worried about lions, he was fearful of men. He also sealed it with the ring of his nobles, in order to avoid all ground for suspicion so far as they were concerned.

Verse 18. "And the king departed to his own house, and went to bed without partaking of supper. ..." How sincere was the king's good will, when he would not touch food night or day or grant his eyelids sleep, but as long as the prophet was in danger he himself remained in a state of sympathetic suspense. But if a king who knew not God did such a thing for another man whose deliverance he desired, how much more ought we to implore God's mercy for our own sins with fastings and watchings.

Verse 19. "Then the king arose at the break of dawn and proceeded with haste to the pit of lions." The term "pit" (lacus) implies a really deep depression, or dry cistern, in which the lions were fed. And so he proceeded hastily to the pit at the break of dawn, believing that Daniel was alive. But in Latin the word lacus is applied to a body of fresh water, such as Lake Benacus [the modern Garda] and Lake Larius [now Lake Como], and the rest of them. The Greeks call it limne, that is, "a body of standing water" (stagnum).

Verse 20. "And approaching the pit, he called out to Daniel with a tear-choked voice and addressed him." By his tears he showed his inner emotion, and forgetting his royal dignity, the conqueror ran to his captive, the master to his servant.

Verse 20b. " 'O Daniel, servant of the living God....'" He calls Him the living God in order to distinguish Him from the gods of the Gentiles, who are but effigies of the dead.

" 'Dost thou deem that thy God, whom thou ever servest, has been able to deliver thee from the lions?' " It was not that he had any doubts about the power of the God of whom he had previously affirmed, "Thy God, whom thou ever servest, will Himself deliver thee." But he phrased the sentence doubtfully in order that when Daniel [reading "Daniel" instead of the meaningless ablative "Daniele"] made his appearance unharmed, the king's anger at the princes might seem the more justified, in proportion to the incredibility of the event.

Verse 21. "'O king, live forever!'" Daniel honors the one who accords honor to him, and prays for him eternal life.

Verse 22. " 'My God sent His angel and shut up the lions' mouths, and they did me no harm.. . .'" The fierceness of the lions was not altered, but their gaping jaws were closed by the angel, and also their voracious hunger, and that too for the reason that the prophet's good works had gone before him. And so his deliverance was not so much a matter of grace as of reward for his unrighteness. And these words might be uttered by every saint, for he has been snatched from the mouths of lions unseen and from the infernal pit, because he has trusted in his God.

Verses 25-27. "Then king Darius wrote unto all the peoples, tribes and language-groups who dwelt in all the earth, saying: (A) 'Your peace be multiplied! I have enacted a decree that in all my empire and kingdom men are to dread and tremble before the God of Daniel. For it is He who is the living God and the One who abides forever, and His rule shall not be overthown, and His power shall eternally endure. It is He who is the Deliverer and Savior, who performs signs and wonders in heaven and on earth, and who has delivered Daniel from the pit of lions.'" Just as in the case of Nebuchadnezzar's writing unto the language-groups and nations one authority has interpreted them to signify hostile powers, so also this same man interprets the action of Darius, on the ground that he summons them all to repentance. And he poses the question as to whether this will take place in this world or in the other world, or even after other worlds have intervened. We deem these speculations to be absurd and account them as empty fables, and make this single observation: that the reason why signs are performed amid barbarian peoples through the agency of God's servants is that the worship and religion of the only God may be proclaimed.

Verse 28. "Thereafter Daniel lived on until the reign of Darius and the reign of Cyrus the Persian." And so the statement which we read above at the end of the first vision, "And Daniel lived until the first year of King Cyrus," is not to be understood as defining the span of his life. In view of the fact that we read in the last vision: "In the third year of Cyrus, King of the Persians, a word was revealed to Daniel, whose surname was Belteshazzar"; this is what is meant, that up to the first year of King Cyrus, who destroyed the empire of the Chaldeans, Daniel continued in power in Chaldea, but was afterwards transferred to Media by Darius.

CHAPTER SEVEN

Verse 1. "In the first year of Belshazzar, King [reading regis for regias] of Babylon, Daniel beheld a dream. And a vision of his head [came to him] upon his bed. And when he wrote the dream down, he comprehended it in a few words and gave a brief summary of it, saying. . .." This section which we now undertake to explain, and also the subsequent section which we are going to discuss, is historically prior to the two previous sections [i.e., chap. 5 and chap. 6]. For this present section and that which follows it are recorded to have taken place in the first and third years of the reign of King Belshazzar (Jer. 39). [Jerome's citation of Jer. 39 seems quite pointless in this connection.] But the section which we read previously to the one just preceding this [i.e., chap. 5], is recorded to have taken place in the last year, indeed on the final day, of Belshaz-zar's reign. And we meet this phenomenon not only in Daniel but also in Jeremiah [cf. Jer. 35 and Jer. 34] and Ezekiel (Ezek. 17), as we shall be able to show, if life spares us that long. But in the earlier portion of the book, the historical order has been followed, namely the events which occurred in the time of Nebuchadnezzar, and Belshazzar, and Darius or Cyrus. But in the passages now before us an account is given of various visions which were beheld on particular occasions and of which only the prophet himself was aware, and which therefore lacked any importance as signs or revelations so far as the barbarian nations were concerned. But they were written down only that a record of the things beheld might be preserved for posterity.

Verses 2, 3. "And during the night I saw in my vision, and behold, the four winds of heaven strove upon the great sea, and four great beasts were coming up out of the sea, differing from one another." The four winds of heaven I suppose to have been angelic powers to whom the principalities have been committed, in accordance with what we read in Deuteronomy: "When the Most High divided the nations and when He separated the children of Adam, He established the bounds of the peoples according to the number of the angels. [Jerome here follows uncritically the Septuagint, which read benev 'el ("sons of God") instead of the Massoretic beney Yisra'el ("sons of Israel"). Since in his own Vulgate translation Jerome followed the Massoretic text and rendered filiorum Israel, he must have written this Commentary before he translated the Pentateuch.] For the Lord's portion is His people; Jacob is the line of His inheritance (B) (Deut. 32:8). But the sea signifies this world and the present age, overwhelmed with salty and bitter waves, in accordance with the Lord's own interpretation of the dragnet cast into the sea (Matt. 13). Hence also the sovereign of all creatures that inhabit the waters is described as a dragon, and his heads, according to David, are smitten in the sea (Ps. 73). And in Amos we read: "If he descends to the very depth of the sea, there will I give him over to the dragon and he shall bite him" (Amos 9:3). But as for the four beasts who came up out of the sea and were differentiated from one another, we may identify them from the angel's discourse. "These four great beasts," he says, "are four kingdoms which shall rise up from the earth." And as for the four winds which strove in the great sea, they are called winds of heaven because each one of the angels does for his realm the duty entrusted to him. This too should be noted, that the fierceness and cruelty of the kingdoms concerned are indicated by the term "beasts."

Verse 4. "The first beast was like a lioness and possessed the wings of an eagle. I beheld until her wings were torn away, and she was raised upright from the ground and stood on her feet like a human being, and she was given a human heart." The kingdom of the Babylonians was not called a lion but a lioness, on account of its brutality and cruelty, or else because of its luxurious, lust-serving manner of life. [Actually Jerome errs in rendering 'aryeh as lioness, for it is the regular masculine form for "lion" in Aramaic, "lioness" being 'aryuta'. Perhaps Jerome mistook the he in the unpointed text before him as the common feminine ending----ah. Or else he simply relied uncritically upon the Septuagint, which commits the same error.] For writers upon the natural history of beasts assert that lionesses are fiercer than lions, especially if they are nursing their cubs, and constantly are passionate in their desire for sexual relations. And as for the fact that she possessed eagle's wings, this indicates the pride of the all-powerful kingdom, the ruler of which declares in Isaiah: "Above the stars of heaven will I place my throne, and I shall be like unto the Most High" (Isa. 14). Therefore he is told: "Though thou be borne on high like an eagle, thence will I drag thee down" (Obad.). Moreover, just as the lion occupies kingly rank among beasts, so also the eagle among the birds. But it should also be said that the eagle enjoys a long span of life, and that the kingdom of Assyrians had held sway for many generations. And as for the fact that the wings of the lioness or eagle were torn away, this signifies the other kingdoms over which it had ruled and soared about in the world. "And she was raised up," he says, "from the ground"; which means, of course (C), that the Chaldean empire was overthrown. And as for what follows, "And she stood upon her feet like a human being, and she was given a human heart," if we understand this as applying to Nebuchadnezzar, it is very evident that after he lost his kingdom and his power had been taken away from him, and after he was once more restored to his original state, he not only learned to be a man instead of a lioness but he also received back the heart which he had lost. But if on the other hand this is to be understood as applying in a general way to the kingdom of the Chaldeans, then it signifies that after Belshazzar was slain [reading interfecto for the impossible inperfecto of the text], and the Medes and Persians succeeded to imperial power, then the men of Babylon realized that theirs was a frail and lowly nature after all. Note the order followed here: the lioness is equivalent to the golden head of the image [in chap. 2].

Verse 5. "And behold another beast like a bear stood up on one side; and there were three rows in his mouth and in his teeth; and they said to him: 'Arise up and devour flesh in abundance.' " The second beast resembling a bear is the same as that of which we read in the vision of the statue (2:32): "His chest and arms were of silver." In the former case the comparison was based on the hardness of the metal, in this case on the ferocity of the bear. For the Persian kingdom followed a rigorous and frugal manner of life after the manner of the Spartans, and that too to such an extent that they used to use salt and nasturtium-cress in their relish. Let us consult the record of the childhood of Cyrus the Great (i.e., "The Education or Training" of Cyrus) [Jerome refers here to Xenophon's "Cyropaideia"]. And as for the fact that the bear is said to have "stood up on one side," the Hebrews interpret it by saying that the Persians never perpetrated any cruelty against Israel. Hence, they are described in the Prophecy of Zechariah also as white horses (Zech. 1). But as for the three rows or ranks that were in his mouth and between his teeth, one authority has interpreted this to mean that allusion was made to the fact that the Persian kingdom was divided up among three princes, just as we read in the sections dealing with Belshazzar and with Darius that there were three princes who were in charge of the one hundred and twenty satraps. But other commentators affirm that these were three kings of the Persians who were subsequent to Cyrus, and yet they fail to mention them by name (A). But we know that after Cyrus's reign of thirty years his son Cambyses ruled among the Persians, and his brothers the magi [the plural seems unwarranted, since there was but one brother involved, namely, Smerdis], and then Darius, in the second year of whose reign the rebuilding of the Temple was commenced at Jerusalem. The fifth king was Xerxes, the son of Darius; the sixth was Artabanus [actually only the assassin of Xerxes; he never became king]; the seventh, Artaxerxes who was surnamed Makrokheir, that is Longimanus ("Long-handed"); the eighth, (B) Xerxes; the ninth, Sogdianus [the reigns of the last two totaled no more than eight months]; the tenth, Darius surnamed Nothos ("Bastard"); the eleventh, the Artaxerxes called Mnemon, that is, "The Rememberer"; the twelfth, the other Artaxerxes, who himself received the surname of Ochus; the thirteenth, Arses, the son of Ochus; and the fourteenth, Darius the son of Arsamus, who was conquered by Alexander, the king of the Macedonians. How then can we say that these were three kings of the Persians? Of course, we could select some who were especially cruel, but we cannot ascertain them on the basis of the historical accounts. Therefore, the three rows in the mouth of the Persian kingdom and between its teeth we must take to be the three kingdoms of the Babylonians, the Medes, and the Persians, all of which were reduced to a single realm. And as for the information, "And thus they spake to him: 'Devour flesh in abundance,' " this refers to the time when in the reign of the Ahasuerus whom the Septuagint calls Artaxerxes, the order was given, at the suggestion of Haman the Agagite, that all the Jews be slaughtered on a single day (Esth. 3). And very properly, instead of saying, "He was devouring them" the account specifies, "Thus they spake unto him...." This shows that the matter was only attempted, and was by no means ever carried out.

Verse 6. "After this I beheld, and lo, there was another beast (C) like unto a leopard, and it had jour wings of a bird all its own [?the per se here is obscure], and there were four heads to the beast, and power was given to it." The third kingdom was that of the Macedonians, of which we read in connection with the image, "The belly and thighs were of bronze." It is compared to a leopard because it is very swift and hormetikos [impetuous], and it charges headlong to shed blood, and with a single bound rushes to its death. "And it had four wings...." There was never, after all, any victory won more quickly than Alexander's, for he traversed all the way from Illyricum and the Adriatic Sea to the Indian Ocean and the Ganges River, not merely fighting battles but winning decisive victories; and in six years he subjugated to his rule a portion of Europe and all of Asia. And by the four heads reference is made to his generals who subsequently rose up as successors to his royal power, namely Ptolemy, Seleucus, Philip [i.e., Philip Arrhidaeus, an illegitimate brother of Alexander, who was proclaimed king upon Alexander's death, but never exercised genuine power, and died after seven years], and Antigonus [the precursor of Seleucus in the rule of the Asiatic portion of Alexander s empire]. "And power was given to it" shows that the empire did not result from Alexander's bravery but from the will of God.

Verse 7. "After this, I beheld in the night-vision, and behold, there was a fourth beast, terrible and wonderful and exceedingly strong. He had large iron teeth, devouring and crushing, and everything that was left he stamped to pieces under his feet." The fourth empire is the Roman Empire, which now occupies the entire world, and concerning which it was said in connection with the image, "Its lower legs were of iron, and part of its feet were of iron, and part of clay." And yet from the iron portion itself Daniel calls to mind that its teeth were iron, and solemnly avers that they were large in size. I find it strange that although he had set forth a lioness, a bear and a leopard in the case of the three previous kingdoms, he did not compare the Roman realm to any sort of beast. Perhaps it was in order to render the beast fearsome indeed that he gave it no name, intending thereby that we should understand the Romans to partake of all the more ferocious characteristics we might think of in connection with beasts. The Hebrews believe that the beast which is here not named is the one spoken of in the Psalms: "A boar from the forest laid her waste, and a strange wild animal consumed her" (Ps. 79:14). [This is the citation according to the Septuagint and Vulgate, whose translation of the Septuagint is here quoted; but the citation in the Hebrew text is Ps. 80:14, and in the English Version, 80:13.] Instead of this the Hebrew reads: "All the beasts of the field have torn her." [A more accurate rendering of the Hebrew would be: ". . .and the moving creatures (or "swarms") of the field do feed upon her."] While they are all included in the one Empire of the Romans, we recognize at the same time those kingdoms which were previously separate. And as for the next statement, ". . .devouring and crushing, and pounding all the rest to pieces under his feet," this signifies that all nations have either been slain by the Romans or else have been subjected to tribute and servitude.

". . .But it did not resemble the other beasts which I had previously seen" (Vulgate: "...which I had seen before it"). In the earlier beasts he had seen various symbols of fright-fulness, but they were all concentrated in this one.

"...and it had ten horns." Porphyry assigned the last two beasts, that of the Macedonians and that of the Romans, to the one realm of the Macedonians and divided them up as follows. He claimed that the leopard was Alexander himself, and that the beast which was dissimilar to the others represented the four successors of Alexander, and then he enumerates ten kings up to the time of Antiochus, surnamed Epiphanes, and who were very cruel. And he did not assign the kings themselves to separate kingdoms, for example Macedon, Syria, Asia, or Egypt, but rather he made out the various kingdoms a single realm consisting of a series. This he did of course in order that the words which were written: "...a mouth uttering overweening boasts" [in the last part of verse 8] might be considered as spoken about Antiochus instead of about Antichrist.

Verse 8. "I was looking at the horns, and behold, another small horn rose up out of the midst of them, and three of the earlier horns were torn away before it. And behold, there were in that horn eyes like unto human eyes, and a mouth uttering overweening boasts." Porphyry vainly surmises that the little horn which rose up after the ten horns is Antiochus Epiphanes, and that the three uprooted horns out of the ten are (A) Ptolemy VI (surnamed Philometer), Ptolemy VII (Euergetes), and Artaraxias, King of Armenia. The first two of these kings died long before Antiochus was born. Against Artarxias, to be sure, we know that Antiochus indeed waged war, but also we know that Artarxias remained in possession of his original kingly authority. We should therefore concur with the traditional interpretation of all the commentators of the Christian Church, that at the end of the world, when the Roman Empire is to be destroyed, there shall be ten kings who will partition the Roman world amongst themselves. Then an insignificant eleventh king will arise, who will overcome three of the ten kings, that is, the king of Egypt, the king of [North] Africa, and the king of Ethiopia, as we shall show more clearly in our later discussion. Then after they have been slain, the seven other kings also will bow their necks to the victor. "And behold," he continues, "there were eyes like unto human eyes in that horn." Let us not follow the opinion of some commentators and suppose him to be either the Devil or some demon, but rather, one of the human race, in whom Satan will wholly take up his residence in bodily form. "...and a mouth uttering overweening boasts..." (cf. II Thess. 2). For this is the man of sin, the son of perdition, and that too to such a degree that he dares to sit in the temple of God, making himself out to be like God.

Verse 9. "I beheld until thrones were set up, and the Ancient of days took His seat. His garment was as white as snow, and the hair of His head was like pure wool. His throne was composed of fiery flames and its wheels were set on fire. From before His presence there issued forth a rushing, fiery stream." We read something similar in John's Apocalypse: (Rev. 4:2 ff.) "After these things I was immediately in the Spirit, and lo, a throne was set up in heaven, and one was seated upon the throne; and He who sat upon it had the likeness of jasper and sardine stone, and there was a rainbow round about the throne like the appearance of emerald. Around the throne there were twenty-four other thrones, and upon the twenty-four thrones there sat twenty-four elders, clothed in shining garments; upon their heads was a golden crown (B), and lightning flashes issued from the throne, and voices and thunder. And in front of the throne there were seven torches of burning fire, which were the seven spirits of God. And in front of the throne lay a glassy sea like unto crystal." And so the many thrones which Daniel saw seem to me to be what John called the twenty-four thrones. And the Ancient (C) of days is the One who, according to John sits alone upon His throne. Likewise the Son of man, who came unto the Ancient of days, is the same as He who, according to John, is called the Lion of the tribe of Judah (Rev. 5), the Root of David, and the titles of that sort. I imagine that these thrones are the ones of which the Apostle Paul says, "Whether thrones or dominions. . ." (Col. 1:16). And in the Gospel we read, "Ye yourselves shall sit upon twelve thrones, judging the twelve tribes of Israel" (Matt. 10:28). And God is called the One who sits and who is the Ancient of days, in order that His character as eternal Judge might be indicated. His garment is shining white like the snow, and the hair of His head is like pure wool. The Savior also, when He was transfigured on the mount and assumed the glory of His divine majesty, appeared in shining white garments (Matt. 17). And as for the fact that His hair is compared to perfectly pure wool, the even-handedness and uprightness of His judgment is shown forth, a judgment which shows no partiality in its exercise. Moreover He is described as an elderly man, in order that the ripeness of His judgment may be established. His throne consists of fiery flames, in order that sinners may tremble before the severity of the torments [of hell], and also that the just may be saved, but so as by fire. The wheels of the throne are set aflame, or else it is the wheels of His chariot which are aflame. In Ezekiel also God is ushered on the scene seated in a four-horse chariot (Ez. 1), and everything pertaining to God is of a fiery consistency. In another place also a statement is made on this subject: "God is a consuming fire" (Deut. 4:24), that we might know that wood, hay and stubble are going to burn up in the day of judgment. And in the Psalms we read: "Fire goeth before Him, and He shall set aflame all His enemies round about Him" (Ps. 96:3). A rushing, fiery stream proceeded from before Him in order that it might carry sinners to hell (Gehenna).

Verse 10. "There were millions ministering unto Him, and a billion stood by His side." [The Aramaic original is more conservative: "A million were ministering unto Him, and a hundred million were standing (in His presence)."] This was not intended to be a specific number for the servants of God, but only indicates a multitude too great for human computation These are the thousands and tens of thousands of which we read in the Psalms: "The chariot of God is attended by ten thousands; thousands of them that rejoice. The Lord is among them" (Ps. 67:18). And in another place: "He who maketh His angels spirits, and His ministers a flaming fire" (Ps. 103:4). [The Protestant reader should always add one to the Vulgate Psalm-number in order to arrive at the Psalm-number of the Hebrew Bible or the English Version.] Now the duty of angels is twofold: the duty of one group is to bestow rewards upon just men; the duty of the other is to have charge over individual calamities [i.e., calamities in the lives of individuals? The original is: qui singulis praesunt cruciatibus]. (D)

". ... The court was in session, and the books were opened." The consciences of men, and the deeds of individuals which partake of either character, whether good or bad, are disclosed to all. One of the books is the good book of which we often read, namely the book of the living. The other is the evil book which is held in the hand of the accuser, who is the fiend and avenger of whom we read in Revelation: "The accuser of our brethren" (Rev. 12:10). This is the earthly book of which the prophet says: "Let them be written on earth" (Jer. 17:13).

Verse 11. "I looked on because of the sound of the lofty words which that horn was uttering." The judgment of God descends for the humbling of pride. Hence the Roman Empire also will be destroyed, because [it is] the horn [which] was uttering the lofty words.

". . .And I saw that the beast was slain and its body perished." In the one empire of the Romans, all the kingdoms at once are to be destroyed, because of the blasphemy of the Antichrist. And the [succeeding] empire shall not be an earthly empire at all, but it is simply the abode of the saints which is spoken of here, and the advent of the conquering Son of God.

Verses 13, 14. "And behold, there came One with the clouds of heaven like unto the Son of man." He who was described in the dream of Nebuchadnezzar as a rock cut without hands, which also grew to be a large mountain, and which smashed the earthenware, the iron, the bronze, the silver, and the gold is now introduced as the very person of the Son of man, so as to indicate in the case of the Son of God how He took upon Himself human flesh; according to the statement which we read in the Acts of the Apostles: "Ye men of Galilee, why stand ye gazing up towards heaven? This Jesus who has been taken up from you into heaven, shall so come in like manner as ye have seen Him going into heaven" (Acts 1:11).

". . .And He arrived unto the Ancient of days, and they brought Him before His presence, and He gave unto Him authority and honor and royal power." All that is said here concerning His being brought before Almighty God and receiving authority and honor and royal power is to be understood in the light of the Apostle's statement: "Who, although He was in the form of God, thought it not robbery to be equal with God; but emptied Himself, taking the form of a servant, being made in the likeness of men, and was found in His condition to be as a man: He humbled Himself, becoming obedient unto death, even to the death of the cross" (Phil. 2:6-8). And if the sect of the Arians were willing to give heed to all this Scripture with a reverent mind, they would never direct against the Son of God the calumny that He is not on an equality with God.

".. .And He is the one whom all the peoples, tribes, and language-groups shall serve. His authority is an eternal authority which shall not be removed, and His kingdom shall be one that shall never be destroyed... ." Let Porphyry answer the query of whom out of all mankind this language might apply to, or who this person might be who was so powerful as to break and smash to pieces the little horn, whom he interprets to be Antiochus? If he replies that the princes of Antiochus were defeated by Judas Maccabaeus, then he must explain how Judas could be said to come with the clouds of heaven like unto the Son of man, and to be brought unto the Ancient of days, and how it could be said that authority and royal power was bestowed upon him, and that all peoples and tribes and language-groups served him, and that his power is eternal and not terminated by any conclusion.

Verses 17, 18. "These four great beasts are the four kingdoms which shall arise from the earth. But the saints of the Most High God shall take the kingdom." The four kingdoms of which we have spoken above were earthly in character. "For everything which is of the earth shall return to earth" (Eccl. 3:20). But the saints shall never possess an earthly kingdom, but only a heavenly. Away, then, with the fable about a millennium! [Cesset ergo mille annorum fabula.]

"...And they shall possess the kingdom unto eternity, even forever and ever. ..." If this be taken to refer to the Maccabees, the advocate of this position should explain how the kingdom of the Maccabees is of a perpetual character.

Verse 25. "And he shall utter (variant: "he utters") speeches against the Lofty One." Or else, as Symmachus has rendered it: "He utters speeches like God," so that one who assumes the authority of God will also arrogate to himself the words of divine majesty.

"...And he shall crush the saints of the Most High, and will suppose himself to be able to alter times and laws." The Antichrist will wage war against the saints and will overcome them; and he shall exalt himself to such a height of arrogance (A) as to attempt changing the very laws of God and the sacred rites as well. He will also lift himself up against all that is called God, subjecting all religion to his own authority.

"...And they shall be delivered into his hand for a time, and times, and half a time." "Time" is equivalent to "year." The word "times," according to the idiom of the Hebrews (who also possess the dual number) represents "two years." [The Aramaic original here, according to the Massoretic vowel pointing, has the plural ending ----iyn, not the dual ending ----ayin. To be sure, the consonantal text could also be pointed as dual.] The half a year signifies "six months." During this period the saints are to be given over to the power of the Antichrist, in order that those Jews might be condemned who did not believe the truth but supported a lie. The Savior also speaks of this period in the Gospel, saying: "Unless those days had been cut short, no flesh would be saved" (Matt. 24:22). In the final vision we shall assert the inappropriateness of this period to Antiochus.

Verse 26. "And the court will sit in judgment, that (Antichrist's) power may be taken away and be crushed in pieces and utterly perish even unto the end." This refers to Antichrist, that is, to the little horn which uttered the lofty words, for his kingdom is to be permanently destroyed.

Verse 27. "But kingdom and power and a vast realm comprising all that is under heaven shall be conferred upon the nation of the saints of the Most High, whose kingdom is an eternal kingdom, and whom all kings shall serve and obey." Here the reference is to Christ's empire, which is eternal.

Verse 28. "Thus far is the end of the word." That is, "the end of that word and discourse which the Lord revealed to me in this present vision."

"...I, Daniel, was much troubled with my thoughts (B), and my countenance was altered within me; but I preserved the word in my heart." Up to this point the Book of Daniel was written in the Chaldee and Syriac language. All the rest that follows up to the very end of the volume we read in Hebrew.

CHAPTER EIGHT
Verse 1. "In the third year of the reign of King Belshazzar, a vision appeared to me. I, Daniel, after what I had seen at the first. ..." This vision came two years after the previous revelation, for the latter was beheld in the first year of Belshazzar, whereas this was beheld in the third year. And so he informs us: "...after that which I had seen at the first."

Verse 2. "I saw in my vision while I was in the castle of Susa, which is in the region of Elam" (Vulgate: "city of Elam"). Or else we may render, as Symmachus has translated it, ".. .in the city of Elam," from which of course the region took its name, just as the Babylonians were named from Babylon. So also the Elamites were thus named from Elam, in consequence of which the Septuagint translates it: "the region of Elamais." And Susis [that is, "Susa"] is the chief city of the region of the Elamites, and there, according to Josephus' account (A), Daniel erected a lofty tower fashioned of square blocks of marble, and of such outstanding beauty that it seems newly built even up to the present day. There also the remains of the kings of the Persians and Medes lie buried, and the custodian or sacristan and priest of that locality is a Jew. "While I was in the castle at Susa. ..." Not that the city itself is a castle, for as we have stated, it is a chief city of great power; but rather that the city is so solidly built that it looks like a castle.

"And I saw in the vision that I was over the gate of Ulai." Instead of this Aquila translated:". . .over the Ubal of Ulai"; Theodotion rendered: "above Ubal"; Symmachus: "above the swamp of Ulai"; the Septuagint: (B) "above the gate of Ulai." But it should be understood that Ulai is the name of a place, or else of a gate, just as there was in Troy a gate called the Skaia ["Western"], and among the Romans there is one called Carmentalis. In each case the name has originated from special circumstances. [Actually the Hebrew word " 'uwbal" is a common noun meaning "canal"; the proper translation would be: "I was by the Ulai Canal."]

Verse 3. "And I lifted up my eyes and saw." Yet of course one only sees in dreams things which appear as shadowy representations, naturally, and as mere likenesses, rather than our being able to behold the reality of the objects themselves (C).

"And behold, a ram stood in front of the swamp (or: in front of the gate ---- the word being UBAL in the Hebrew), having lofty horns, one of which was higher than the other and growing yet larger." He calls Darius, Cyrus's uncle, a ram. He reigned over the Medes after his father, Astyages. And the one horn which was higher than the other, and growing still larger, signified Cyrus himself, who succeeded his maternal grandfather, Astyages, and reigned over the Medes and Persians along with his uncle, Darius, whom the Greeks called Cyaxeres.

Verse 4. "After this I saw the ram pushing with its horns westward (D) and northward and southward...." Not that he saw the ram itself, that is, the ram of Cyrus or Darius, but rather the ram of the same kingdom as theirs, that is, the second Darius, who was the last king of the Persian power, and who was overcome by the king of the Macedonians, Alexander the son of Philip. And as to the fact that Darius was a very powerful and wealthy king, both the Greek and the Latin and the barbarian historical accounts so relate.

Verse 5. "And I myself understood. ..." On the basis of the previous visions which had symbolized the second kingdom by the ram and the he-goat, Daniel now also understood that he was looking at the empire of the Medes and Persians.

"And behold, there was a he-goat which was coming from the West above the surface of the whole earth, and yet without touching the ground. ..." So that no one will think that I am attaching a private interpretation to this, let us simply repeat the words of Gabriel as he explained the prophet's vision. He said, "The ram whom thou sawest to possess two horns is the king of the Medes and Persians." This was, of course, Darius the son of Arsames, in whose reign the kingdom of the Medes and Persians was destroyed. "There was in addition a he-goat, who was coming from the west," and because of his extraordinary speed he appeared not to touch the ground. This was Alexander, the king of the Greeks, who after the overthrow of Thebes took up arms against the Persians. Commencing the conflict at the Granicus River, he conquered the generals of Darius and finally smashed against the ram himself and broke in pieces his two horns, the Medes and the Persians. Casting him beneath his feet, he subjected both horns to his own authority.

"And (he had) a large horn. ..." refers to the first king, Alexander himself. When he died in Babylon at the age of thirty-two, his four generals rose up in his place and divided his empire among themselves. For Ptolemy, the son of Lagos, seized Egypt; the Philip who was also called Aridaeus (var.: Arius), the (half-) brother of Alexander took over Macedonia; Seleucus Nicanor took over Syria, Babylonia, and all the kingdoms of the East; and Antigonus ruled over Asia Minor. "But (they shall not rise up) with his power" (chap. 8:22), since no one was able to equal the greatness of Alexander himself. "And a long time afterward" there shall arise "a king of Syria who shall be of shameless countenance and shall understand (evil) counsels," even Antiochus Epiphanes, the son of the Seleucus who was also called Philopator.

Verse 9. After he had been a hostage to Rome, and had without the knowledge of the Senate obtained rule by treachery, Antiochus fought with Ptolemy Philometor, that is, "against the South" and against Egypt; and then again "against the East," and against those who were fomenting revolution in Persia. At the last he fought against the Jews and captured Judea, entering into Jerusalem and setting up in the Temple of God the statue of Jupiter Olympius. "...and against the power of heaven," that is, against the children of Israel, who were protected by the assistance of angels. He pushed his arrogance to such an extreme that he subjected the majority of the saints to the worship of idols, as if he would tread the very stars beneath his feet. And thus it came to pass that he held the South and the East, that is, Egypt and Persia, under his sway.

Verses 11, 12. And as for the statement, "And he glorified himself even against the Prince of Power," this means that he lifted himself up against God and persecuted His saints. He even took away the endelekhismos or "continual offering" which was customarily sacrificed in the morning and at even, and he prevailed to the casting down of the "place of His sanctuary." And he did not do this by his own prowess, but only "on account of the sins of the people." And thus it came to pass that truth was prostrated upon the ground, and as the worship of idols flourished, the religion of God suffered an eclipse.

Verse 13. "And I heard one of the saints speaking, and one saint said to another saint (I do not know which one), who was conversing with him." Instead of "another one which one I do not know" ---- the rendering of Symmachus (A) (tini pote) which I too have followed ---- Aquila and Theodotion, and the Septuagint as well, have simply put the Hebrew word (p-l-m-n-y) phelmoni (B) itself. Without specifying the angel's name, I should say that the author indicated some one of the angels or other in a general way.

" 'How long shall be the vision concerning the continual sacrifice and the sin of the desolation that is made, and the sanctuary and the strength be trodden under foot?'" One angel asks another angel for how long a period the Temple is by the judgment of God to be desolated under the rule of Antiochus, King of Syria, and how long the image of Jupiter is to stand in God's Temple (according to his additional statement: "... and the sanctuary and the strength be trodden under foot?").

Verse 14. And he answered him, " 'Until the evening and the morning, until two thousand three hundred days (C); and then the sanctuary shall be cleansed.' " If we read the Books of Maccabees and the history of Josephus, we shall find it there recorded that in the one hundred and forty-third year after the Seleucus who first reigned in Syria after the decease of Alexander, Antiochus entered Jerusalem, and after wreaking a general devastation he returned again in the third year and set up the statue of Jupiter in the Temple. Up until the time of Judas Macca-baeus, that is, up until the one hundred and eighth year, Jerusalem lay waste over a period of six years, and for three [of those] years the Temple lay defiled; making up a total of two thousand three hundred days plus three months. [At least that is what the text seems to say, following the present word-order. Actually the three months should be added to the six years in order to come out to a total of approximately 2300 days.] At the end of the period the Temple was purged. Some authorities read two hundred instead of two thousand three hundred, in order to avoid the apparent excess involved in six years and three months. [Actually, however, 2200 days would come out to only six years and nine days; the reasoning here seems obscure.] Most of our commentators refer this passage to the Antichrist, and hold that that which occurred under Antiochus was only by way of a type which shall be fulfilled under Antichrist. And as for the statement, "The sanctuary shall be cleansed," this refers to the time of Judas Maccabaeus, who came from the village of Modin, and who being aided by the efforts of his brothers (D) and relatives and many of the Jewish people [defeated?] [the verb is left out] the generals of Antiochus not far above Emmaus (which is now called Nicopolis). And hearing of this, Antiochus, who had risen up against the Prince of princes, that is, against the Lord of lords and King of kings, was earnestly desirous of despoiling the temple of Diana which was located in Elimais, in the Persian district, because it possessed valuable votive offerings. And when he there lost his army, he was destroyed without hands, that is to say, he died of grief. As for the mention of evening and morning [in that fourteenth verse], this signifies the succession of day and night.

Verse 15. "And it came to pass that when I, Daniel, had seen the vision, I sought to understand it." He beheld the vision by way of a picture or likeness, and he failed to understand it. Consequently, not everyone who sees comprehends what he has seen; it is just as if we read the Holy Scripture with our eyes and do not understand it with our heart,

"...And behold, one stood before me who resembled the appearance of a man." Angels, after all, are not actually men by nature, but they resemble men in appearance. For example, three persons appeared as men to Abraham at the oak of Mamre (Gen. 18), and yet they certainly were not men, for one of them was worshipped as the Lord. And so the Savior also stated in the Gospel: "Abraham beheld My day; he beheld it and rejoiced" (John 8:56).

Verses 16, 17. "And I heard the voice of a man in the midst of the Ulai, and he cried out and said: 'Gabriel, make this vision intelligible (Vulgate: make this man to understand the vision).' And he came and stood near to where I was standing." The Jews claim that this man who directed Gabriel to explain the vision to Daniel was Michael [himself]. Quite appropriately it was Gabriel, who has been put in charge of battles, to whom this duty was assigned, inasmuch as the vision had to do with battles and contests between kings and even between kingdoms themselves. For Gabriel is translated into our language as "the strength of, or the mighty one of, God." And so at that time also when the Lord was about to be born and to declare war against the demons and to triumph over the world, Gabriel came to Zacharias and to Mary (Luke 1). And then we read in the Psalms concerning the Lord in His triumph: "Who is this king of glory? The Lord strong and mighty, the Lord mighty in battle; He is the King of glory" (Ps. 23:8=24:8). [The point of this quotation seems to be that the Hebrew word for "mighty" is gibbowr, from the root of which comes the gabri- of Gabriel.] But whenever it is medicine or healing that is needed, it is Raphael who is sent, for his name is rendered as "the healing of," or "the medicine of God" (E)---- that is, if one cares to accept the authority of the Book of Tobias. And then, when favorable promises are made to the people, and hilasmos, which we might render as "propitiation" or "expiation," is the thing required (F), then it is Michael who is directed to go, for his name means, "Who is like God?" Of course the significance of the name indicates the fact that the only true remedy is to be found in God.

"And he said to me: 'Son of man, understand that in the time of the end the vision shall be fulfilled.'" Inasmuch as Ezekiel and Daniel and Zechariah behold themselves to be often in the company of angels, they were reminded of their frailty, lest they should be lifted up in pride and imagine themselves to partake of the nature or dignity of angels. Therefore they are addressed **as sons of men, in order that they might realize that they are but human beings.**

Verses 18, 19. "And he touched me and stood me upon my feet, and said to me. .. ." Overcome with terror, the prophet was lying on the ground face downward upon his hands and knees, but at the angel's touch he was raised up to a standing position in order that he might without perturbation attend to and understand what was spoken.

Verse 26. "Thou therefore seal up the vision, because it shall come to pass after many days." Having explained the vision which we have examined above to the best of our ability, the angel Gabriel adds at the end: "Thou therefore seal up the vision, because it shall come to pass after many days." By the mention of a seal, he showed that the things spoken were of a hidden character and not accessible to the ears of the multitude, or susceptible of comprehension prior to their actual fulfilment by the events themselves.

Verse 27. "And I, Daniel, languished and was sick for some days. And when I rose from my bed, I performed the king's tasks." This is the same thing as we read in Genesis about Abraham, for after he had heard the Lord speaking to him, he averred that he was but dust and ashes (Gen. 18). And so Daniel states that he languished as a reaction to the horror of the vision, and suffered illness. And after he had risen from his sick-bed, he says he performed the tasks assigned to him by the king, rendering to all men all that was due them and bearing in mind the gospel principle: "Render unto Caesar the things that are Caesar's, and to God the things that are God's" (Luke 20:25).

"And I was amazed at the vision, and there was no one who could interpret it." If there was no one who could interpret it, how was it that the angel interpreted it in the previous passage? What he means is that he had heard mention of kings and did not know what their names were; he learned of things to come, but he was tossed about with uncertainty as to what time they would come to pass. And so he did the only thing he could do: he marveled at the vision, and resigned everything to God's omniscience.

CHAPTER NINE

Verses 1, 2. "In the first year of the Darius who was the son of Ahasuerus of the race of the Medes and who reigned over the kingdom of the Chaldeans, in the first year of his reign. ..." This is the Darius who in cooperation with Cyrus conquered the Chaldeans and Babylonians. We are not to think of that other Darius in the second year of whose reign the Temple was built (as Porphyry supposes in making out a late date for Daniel); nor are we to think of the Darius who was vanquished by Alexander, the king of the Macedonians. He therefore adds the name of his father and also refers to his victory, inasmuch as he was the first of the race of the Medes to overthrow the kingdom of the Chaldeans. He does this to avoid any mistake in the reading which might arise from the similarity of the name.

Verse 2. "I, Daniel, understood by the books the number of the years concerning which the word of the Lord had come to the prophet Jeremiah, that seventy years would be accomplished for the desolation of Jerusalem." Jeremiah had predicted seventy years for the desolation of the Temple (Jer. 52:29), at the end of which the people would again return to Judaea and build the Temple and the city of Jerusalem. But this fact did not render Daniel careless, but rather encouraged him to pray that God might through his supplications fulfil that which He had graciously promised. Thus he avoided the danger that carelessness might result in pride, and pride cause offense to the Lord. Accordingly we read in Genesis (chap. 9) [sic!] that prior to the Deluge one hundred and twenty years were appointed for men to come to repentance; and inasmuch as they refused to repent even within so long an interval of time as a hundred years, God did not wait for the remaining twenty years to be fulfilled, but brought on the punishment earlier which He had threatened for a later time. [This deduction seems to have been based upon the fact that Gen. 5:32 mentions that Noah was five hundred years old when he had begotten Ham, Shem, and Japheth, and therefore was still the same age when God appointed the one hundred twenty years in Gen. 6:3. Since the Flood dried up in the six hundred and first year of Noah (8:13), therefore the waiting period could not have been more than a hundred years. Yet it could also have been that the age given in Gen. 5:32 was the age when, within the one hundred twenty year period, Noah's family was complete, the youngest son being born within that period, and being old enough to be married by the time the Flood itself actually occurred.] So also Jeremiah is told, on account of the hardness of the heart of the Jewish people: "Pray not for this people, for I will not hearken unto thee" (Jer. 7:16). Samuel also was told: "How long wilt thou mourn over Saul? I also have rejected him" (I Sam. 16:1). And so it was with sackcloth and ashes that Daniel besought the Lord to fulfil what He had promised, not that Daniel lacked faith concerning the future, but rather he would avoid the danger that a feeling of security might produce carelessness, and carelessness produce an offense to God.

Verse 4. "'I beseech Thee, O Lord God, who art mighty and terrible....'" That is, Thou art terrible towards those who despise Thine injunctions.

"'...Who keepest covenant and mercy towards those who love Thee and keep Thy commandments.' " It is not therefore the case that what God promises will come to pass without further ado, but rather, He fulfils His promises towards those who keep His commandments.

Verse 5. " 'We have sinned, we have behaved wickedly (A) and impiously, and we have departed....'" He reviews the sins of the people as if he were personally guilty, on the ground of his being one of the people, just as we read the Apostle does also in his Epistle to the Romans.

Verse 7. " 'Justice belongeth unto Thee, O Lord, but for us there is only confusion of face. .. .'" It is of course just that we suffer what we deserve.

Verse 8. " 'Unto Thee belongeth mercy, O Lord our God, and also propitiation. . . .' " Concerning the same God of Whom he had previously said, "To Thee, O Lord, belongeth justice," he now says (since the Lord is not only just but also merciful): "To Thee belongeth mercy." He says this in order that he might call upon the Judge to show mercy, after His sentence has been imposed.

Verse 11. "'And (the curse) has come upon us drop by drop.'" That is, Thou hast not poured out upon us all of Thy wrath, for we should not have been able to bear it, but Thou hast poured forth a mere droplet of Thy fury, in order that we might return unto Thee once we have been immeshed in Thy snare.

" 'The malediction and the curse which were written in the book of Moses, the servant of God. ...' " In Deuteronomy we read the curses and blessings of the Lord (Deut. 27), which were afterwards uttered in Mount Gerizim and Ebal upon the righteous and upon the sinners.

Verse 13. "'All this evil has come upon us, and we have not entreated Thy face, O Lord our God, that we might turn back from our iniquities and consider Thy truth.'" Their obduracy was so great that even in the midst of their toils they would not entreat God, and even if they had entreated Him, it would not have been a genuine entreaty, because they had not turned back from their iniquities. Yet to consider the truth of God is equivalent to turning back from iniquity.

Verse 14. " 'And the Lord hath kept watch over the evil and hath brought it upon us. .. .'" Whenever we are rebuked because of our sins, God is keeping watch over us and visiting us with chastenment. But whenever we are left alone by God and we do not suffer judgment but are unworthy of the Lord's rebuke, then He is said to slumber. And so we read in the Psalms as well: "The Lord has risen up as one (B) who was slumbering or as a man out of a drunken sleep" (Ps. 77=78). For our wickedness and iniquity inflames God with wine, and whenever it is rebuked in our case, God is said to be keeping careful watch and to be rising up out of His drunken sleep, in order that we who are drunken with sin may be made to pay careful heed unto righteousness.

Verse 15. "'And now, O Lord our God....'" Daniel remembers God's ancient kindness in order that he may appeal to Him for a similar act of clemency.

Verse 17. "'And show Thy face upon Thy sanctuary, which lies desolate.'" By deed fulfil that which Thou hast promised in word, for the approximate period of desolation has elapsed.

Verse 18. "For Thine own sake, O my God, incline Thine ear and hear; open Thine eyes and behold our desolation ...." This appeal is couched in anthropomorphic language (anthropopathos), with the implication that whenever our prayers are heard, God seems to incline His ear; and whenever God deigns to have regard to us, He appears to open His eyes; but whenever He turns His face away, we appear to be unworthy of attention either from His eyes or His ears.

Verse 20. "Now while I was yet speaking and praying and confessing my sins and the sins of my people, Israel, so as to present (Vulg.: and was presenting) my petitions in the presence of my God on behalf of the holy mountain of my God. ..." And so, as we have pointed out above, he not only thought upon the sins of the people but also upon his own sins, as being one of the people. Or else it was by way of humility, although he had not personally committed sin; his purpose being to obtain pardon by reason of his humility. Observe what he said here: "I was confessing my sins." For there are many passages in Scripture where confession does not imply an expression of repentance so much as an expression of praise to God.

Verse 21. "While I was still speaking in my prayer, behold the man Gabriel, whom I had seen (A) at the beginning of the vision." He calls the previous vision preceding this one the beginning. The effect of his prayer was considerable, and the promise of God was fulfilled which says, "While thou art yet speaking, lo, I am at hand" (Isa. 58:9). And Gabriel appears not as an angel or archangel, but as a man (vir), a term used to indicate the quality of virtue rather than specifying his sex.

". . .he quickly flew to me and touched me at the time of the evening sacrifice." It is stated that he flew, because he had made his appearance as a man. It is said that it was at the time of the evening sacrifice, in order to show that the prophet's prayer had persisted from the morning sacrifice even unto the evening sacrifice, and that God for that reason directed His mercy towards him.

Verse 22. "And He instructed me and spoke to me, saying. ..." The vision was so obscure that the prophet needed the angel's teaching.

" '.. .Now, 0 Daniel, I have come forth that I may instruct thee and that thou mayest understand.'" That is, I have been sent to thee and have come (B) forth, not from the presence of God in the sense of departing from Him, but only in the sense of coming unto thee.

Verse 23. " 'From the very beginning of thy prayers the word went forth and I myself have come to show it to thee, because thou art a man of desires.'" That is, at the time when thou didst begin to ask God, thou didst straightway obtain His mercy, and His decision was put forth. I have therefore been sent to explain to thee the things of which thou art ignorant, inasmuch as thou art a man of desires, that is to say a lovable man, worthy of God's love ---- even as Solomon was called Idida (var: Jedida) or "man of desires." I have been sent because thou art worthy, in recompense for thine affection for God, to be told the secret counsels of God and to have a knowledge of things to come.

" 'Thou therefore pay heed to the word and understand the vision.' " Thus [reading sic instead of si] Daniel is told, "Pay diligent heed, in order that thou mayest hear and understand what thou seest." We too should do this, for our eyes have been blinded by the shadows of ignorance and the darkness of sins.

Verses 24----27. " 'Seventy weeks are shortened upon thy people and upon thy holy city, (C) that transgression may be finished, and sin may have an end, and iniquity may be abolished, and everlasting justice may be brought to bear, and that the vision and prophecy may be fulfilled that the Holy One of the saints may be anointed. Know therefore and take note that from the going forth of the word to build up Jerusalem again, unto Christ the prince, there shall be seven weeks and sixty-two weeks, and the street shall be built again, and the walls, in distressing times. And after sixty-two weeks Christ shall be slain, and ((D) the people that shall deny Him) shall not be His. And a people, with their leader that shall come, shall destroy the city and the sanctuary. And the end thereof shall be devastation, and after the end of the war there shall be the appointed desolation. And he shall confirm the covenant with many in one xveek; and in the middle of the week both victim and sacrifice shall fail. And there shall be in the Temple the abomination of desolation, and the desolation shall continue even unto the consummation and the end.' " Because the prophet had said, "Thou didst lead forth Thy people, and Thy name was pronounced upon Thy city and upon Thy people," Gabriel therefore, as the mouthpiece of God, says by implication: "By no means are they God's people, but only thy people; nor is Jerusalem the holy city of God, but it is only a holy city unto thee, as thou sayest." This is similar to what we read in Exodus also, when God says to Moses, "Descend, for thy people have committed sin" (Ex. 32:7). That is to say, they are not My people, for they have forsaken Me. And so, because thou dost supplicate for Jerusalem and prayest for the people of the Jews, hearken unto that which shall befall thy people in seventy weeks of years, and those things which will happen to thy city.

I realize that this question has been argued over in various ways by men of greatest learning, and that each of them has expressed his views according to the capacity of his own genius. And so, because it is unsafe to pass judgment upon the opinions of the great teachers of the Church and to set one above another, I shall simply repeat the view of each, and leave it to the reader's judgment as to whose explanation ought to be followed. In the fifth volume of his Tempora ["Chronology"], Africanus has this to say concerning the seventy weeks (and I quote him verbatim): "The chapter (E) which we read in Daniel concerning the seventy weeks contains many remarkable details, which require too lengthy a discussion at this point; and so we must discuss only what pertains to our present task, namely that which concerns chronology. There is no doubt but what it constitutes a prediction of Christ's advent, for He appeared to the world at the end of seventy weeks. After Him the crimes were consummated and sin reached its end and iniquity was destroyed. An eternal righteousness also was proclaimed which overcame the mere righteousness of the law; and the vision and the prophecy were fulfilled, inasmuch as the Law and the Prophets endured until the time of (F) John the Baptist (Luke 16), and then the Saint of saints was anointed. And all these things were the objects of hope, prior to Christ's incarnation, rather than the objects of actual possession. Now the angel himself specified seventy weeks of years, that is to say, four hundred and ninety years from the issuing of the word that the petition be granted and that Jerusalem be rebuilt. The specified interval began in the twentieth year of Artaxerxes, King of the Persians; for it was his cupbearer, Nehemiah (Neh. 1), who, as we read in the book of Ezra [the Vulgate reckons Nehemiah as II Esdras], petitioned the king and obtained his request that Jerusalem be rebuilt. And this was the word, or decree, which granted permission for the construction of the city and its encompassment with walls; for up until that time it had lain open to the incursions of the surrounding nations. But if one points to the command of King Cyrus, who granted to all who desired it permission to return to Jerusalem, the fact of the matter is that the high priest Jesus [Jeshua] and Zerubbabel, and later on the priest Ezra, together with the others who had been willing to set forth from Babylon with them, only made an abortive attempt to construct the Temple and the city with its walls, but were prevented by the surrounding nations from completing the task, on the pretext that the king had not so ordered. And thus the work remained incomplete until Nehemiah's time and the twentieth year of King Artaxerxes. Hence the captivity lasted for seventy years prior to the Persian rule. [This last sentence is bracketed by the editor.] At this period in the Persian Empire a hundred and fifteen years had elapsed since its inception, but it was the one hundred and eighty-fifth year from the captivity of Jerusalem when Artaxerxes first gave orders for the walls of Jerusalem to be built. [Actually only 141 years, the interval between 587 B.C. and 446 B.C.] Nehemiah was in charge of this undertaking, and the street was built and the surrounding walls were erected. Now if you compute seventy weeks of years from that date, you can come out to the time of Christ. But if we wish to take any other date (A) as the starting point for these weeks, then the dates will show a discrepancy and we shall encounter many difficulties. For if the seventy weeks are computed from the time of Cyrus and his decree of indulgence which effectuated the release of the Jewish captives, then we shall encounter a deficit of a hundred years and more short of the stated number of seventy weeks [only seventy-eight years, by more recent computation, for Cyrus's decree was given in 538 B.C.]. If we reckon from the day when the angel spoke to Daniel, the deficit would be much greater [actually not more than a few months or a year]. An even greater number of years is added, if you wish to put the beginning of the weeks at the commencement of the captivity. For the kingdom of the Persians endured for two hundred and thirty years until the rise of the Macedonian kingdom; then the Macedonians themselves reigned for three hundred years. From that date until the sixteenth (i.e., the fifteenth) year of Tiberius Caesar, when Christ suffered death, is an interval of sixty [sic!] years [reckoning from the death of Cleopatra, the last of the Macedonian Ptolemies]. All of these years added together come to the number of five hundred and ninety, with the result that a hundred years remain to be accounted for. On the other hand, the interval from the twentieth year of Artaxerxes to the time of Christ completes the figure of seventy weeks, if we reckon according to the lunar computation of the Hebrews, who did not number their months according to the movement of the sun, but rather according to the moon. For the interval from the one hundred fiftieth year of the Persian Empire, when Artaxerxes, as king thereof, attained the twentieth year of his reign (and this was the fourth year of the eighty-third Olympiad), up until the two hundred and second Olympiad (for it was the second year of that Olympiad which was the fifteenth year of Tiberius Caesar) comes out to be the grand total of four hundred seventy-five years. This would result in four hundred ninety Hebrew years, reckoning according to the lunar months as we have suggested. For according to their computation, these years can be made up of months of twenty-nine (variant: twenty-eight) and a half days each. This means that the sun, during a period of four hundred ninety years, completes its revolution in three hundred sixty-five days and a quarter, and this amounts to twelve lunar months for each individual year, with eleven and a fourth days left over to spare. Consequently, the Greeks and Jews over a period of eight years insert three intercalary months (embolimoi). For if you will multiply eleven and a quarter days by eight, you will come out to ninety days, which equal three months. Now if you divide the eight-year periods into four hundred seventy-five years, your quotient will be fifty-nine plus three months. These fifty-nine plus eight-year periods produce enough intercalary months to make up fifteen years, more or less; and if you will add these fifteen years to the four hundred seventy-five years, you will come out to seventy weeks of years, that is, a total of four hundred and ninety years."

Africanus has expressed his views in these very words which we have copied out. Let us pass on to Eusebius Pamphili [the famous church historian, who assumed the cognomen Pamphili in honor of his beloved mentor, Bishop Pamphilus], who in the eighth book of his Euangelike Apodeixis [the full title was Euangelikes Apodeixeos Proparaskeue or "Preparation for the Demonstration of the Gospel"; the Latin title is Praeparatio Evangelica] ventures some such conjecture as this: "It does not seem to me that the seventy weeks have been divided up without purpose, in that seven is mentioned first, and then sixty-two, and then a last week is added, which in turn is itself divided into two parts. For it is written: 'Thou shalt know and understand that from the issuing of the word (command) that the petition be granted and Jerusalem be built until Christ the Prince there shall be seven weeks and sixty-two weeks.' And after the rest which he relates in the intervening section, he states at the end: 'He shall confirm a testimony (covenant) with many during one week.' It is clear that the angel did not detail these things in his reply to no purpose or apart from the inspiration of God. This observation seems to require some cautious and careful reasoning, so that the reader may pay diligent attention and inquire into the cause for this division (variant: vision). But if we must express our own opinion, in conformity with the rest of the interpretation which concerns this present context, in the angel's statement: 'From the issuing of the word that the petition be granted and that Jerusalem be built, until the time of Christ the Prince,' we are only to think of other princes who had charge of the Jewish people subsequent to this prophecy and subsequent to the return from Babylon. That is to say, we are to think of the arkhiereis [high priests] and pontiffs to whom the Scripture attaches the title of christs, by reason of the fact that they have been anointed. The first of these was Jesus [Jeshua] the son of Jehozadak, the high priest, and then the rest who had that office up until the time of the advent of our Lord and Savior. And it is these who are intended by the prophet's prediction when it states: 'From the issuing of the word that the petition be granted and Jerusalem be built even unto Christ the Prince there shall be seven weeks, and sixty-two weeks.' That is to say, the purpose is that seven weeks be counted off, and then afterward sixty-two weeks, which come to a total of four hundred and eighty-three years after the time of Cyrus. And lest we appear to be putting forth a mere conjecture too rashly and without testing the truth of our statements, let us reckon up those who bore office as christs over the people from the time of Jeshua, the son of Jehozadak, until the advent of the Lord; that is to say, those who were anointed for the high priesthood. First, then, as we have already stated, subsequent to Daniel's prophecy, which occurred in the reign of Cyrus, and subsequent to the return of the people from Babylon, Jeshua the son of Jehozadak was the high priest, and together with Zerubbabel, son of Shealtiel, they laid the foundations of the temple. And because the undertaking was hindered by the Samaritans and the other surrounding nations, seven weeks of years elapsed (that is to say, forty-nine years), during which the work on the temple remained unfinished. These weeks are separated by the prophecy from the remaining sixty-two weeks. And lastly, the Jews also followed this view when they said to the Lord in the Gospel-narrative: 'This temple was built over a period of forty-six years, and shalt thou raise it up in three days' (John 2:20). For this was the number of years which elapsed between the first year of Cyrus, who granted to those Jews who so desired the permission to return to their fatherland, and the sixth year of King Darius, in whose reign the entire work upon the temple was finished. [Actually the two dates involved are 538 B.C. and 516 B.C., an interval of only twenty-two years.] Furthermore Josephus added on three more years, during which the periboloi (precincts) and certain other construction left undone were brought to completion; and when these are added to the forty-six years, they come out to forty-nine years, or seven weeks of years. And the remaining sixty-two weeks are computed from the seventh year of Darius. At that time Jeshua the son of Jehozadak, and Zerubbabel (who had already reached his majority) were in charge of the people, and it was in their time that Haggai and Zechariah prophesied. After them came Ezra and Nehemiah from Babylon and constructed the walls of the city during the high priesthood of Joiakim, son of Jeshua, who had the surname of Jehozadak. After him Eliashib succeeded to the priesthood, then Joiada and Johanan after him. Following him there was Jaddua, in whose lifetime Alexander, the king of the Macedonians, founded Alexandria, as (A) Josephus relates in his books of the Antiquities, and actually came to Jerusalem and offered blood-sacrifices in the Temple. Now Alexander died in the one hundred and thirteenth Olympiad, in the two hundred thirty-sixth year of the Persian Empire, which in turn had begun in the first year of the fifty-fifth Olympiad. That was the date when Cyrus, King of the Persians, conquered the Babylonians and Chaldeans. After the death of the priest Jaddua, who had been in charge of the temple in Alexander's reign, Onias received the high priesthood. It was at this period that Seleucus, after the conquest of Babylon, placed upon his own head the crown of all Syria and Asia, in the twelfth year after Alexander's death. Up to that time the years which had elapsed since the rule of Cyrus, when computed together, were two hundred and forty-eight. From that date the Scripture of the Maccabees computes the kingdom of the Greeks. Following Onias, the high priest Eleazar became head of the Jews. That was the period when the Seventy translators (Septuaginta interpretes) are said to have translated the Holy Scriptures into Greek at Alexandria. After him came Onias II, who was followed by Simon, who ruled over the people when Jesus the son of Sirach wrote the book which bears the Greek title of Panaretos ("A Completely Virtuous Man"), and which is by most people falsely attributed to Solomon. Another Onias followed him in the high priesthood, and that was the period when Antiochus was trying to force the Jews to sacrifice to the gods of the Gentiles. After the death of Onias, Judas Maccabaeus cleansed the Temple and smashed to bits the statues of the idols. His brother Jonathan followed him, and after Jonathan their brother Simon governed the people. By his death the two hundred and seventy-seventh year of the Syrian kingdom had elapsed, and the First Book of Maccabees contains a record of events up to that time. And so, the total number of years from the first year of Cyrus, King of Persia, until the end of the First Book of Maccabees and the death of the high priest Simon is four hundred twenty-five. After him John [Hyrcanus] occupied the high priesthood for twenty-nine years, and upon his death Aristobulus became head of the people for a year and was the first man after the return from Babylon to associate with the dignity of high priesthood the authority of kingship. His successor was Alexander, who likewise was high priest and king, and who governed the people for twenty-seven years. Up to this point, the number of years from the first year of Cyrus and the return of the captives who desired to come back to Judaea is to be computed at four hundred and eighty-three. This total is made up of the seven weeks and the sixty-two weeks, or sixty-nine weeks altogether. And during this whole period high priests ruled over the Jewish people, and I now believe that they are those referred to as christ-princes. And when the last of them, Alexander, had died, the Jewish nation was rent in this direction and that into various factions, and was harrassed by internal seditions in its leaderless condition; and that too to such an extent that Alexandra, who was also called Salina, and who was the wife of the same Alexander, seized power and kept the high priesthood for her son, Hyrcanus. But she passed on the royal power to her other son, Aristobulus, and he exercised it for ten years. But when the brothers fought with each other in civil war and the Jewish nation was drawn into various factions, then Gnaeus Pompey, the general of the Roman army, came upon the scene. Having captured Jerusalem, he penetrated even to the shrine in the temple which was called the Holy of holies. He sent Aristobulus back to Rome in chains, keeping him for his triumphal procession, and then he gave the high priesthood to his brother, Hyrcanus. Then for the first time the Jewish nation became tributary to the Romans. Succeeding him, Herod, the son of Antipater, received the royal authority over the Jews by senatorial decree, after Hyrcanus had been killed; and so he was the first foreigner to become governor of the Jews. Moreover when his parents had died, he handed over the high priesthood to his children, even though they were non-Jews, utterly contrary to the law of Moses. Nor did he entrust the office to them for long, (B) except upon their granting him favors and bribes, for he despised the commands of God's law."

The same Eusebius offered another explanation also, and if we wanted to translate it into Latin, we should greatly expand the size of this book. And so the sense of his interpretation is this, that the number of years from the sixth year of Darius, who reigned after Cyrus and his son, Cambyses, ---- and this was the date when the work on the temple was completed ---- until the time of Herod and Caesar Augustus is reckoned to be seven weeks plus sixty-two weeks, which make a total of four hundred eighty-three years. That was the date when the Christ, that is to say, Hyrcanus, being the last high priest of the Maccabaean line, was murdered by Herod, and the succession of high priests came to an end, so far as the law of God was concerned. It was then also that a Roman army under the leadership of a Roman general devastated both the city and the sanctuary itself. Or else it was Herod himself who committed the devastation, after he had through the Romans appropriated to himself a governmental authority to which he had no right. And as for the angel's statement, "For he shall establish a compact with many for one week (variant: "a compact for many weeks"), and in the midst of the week the sacrifice and offering shall cease," it is to be understood in this way, that Christ was born while Herod was reigning in Judaea and Augustus in Rome, and He preached the Gospel for three years and six months, according to John the Evangelist. And he established the worship of the true God with many people, undoubtedly meaning the Apostles and believers generally. And then, after our Lord's passion, the sacrifice and offering ceased in the middle of the week. For whatever took place in the Temple after that date was not a valid sacrifice to God but a mere worship of the devil, while they all cried out together, "His blood be upon us and upon our children" (Matt. 27:25); and again, "We have no king but Caesar." Any reader who is interested may look up this passage in the Chronicle of this same Eusebius, for I translated it into Latin many years ago. But as for his statement that the number of years to be reckoned from the completion of the temple to the tenth year of the Emperor Augustus, that is, when Hyrcanus was slain and Herod obtained Judaea, amounts to a total of seven plus sixty-two weeks, or four hundred eighty-three years, we may check it in the following fashion. The building of the temple was finished in the seventy-sixth (here and in the other place read: "sixty-seventh" ---- Migne) Olympiad, which was the sixth year of Darius. In the third year of the one hundred and eighty-sixth Olympiad, that is, the tenth year of Augustus, Herod seized the rule over the Jews. This makes the interval four hundred and eighty-three years, reckoning up by the individual Olympiads and computing them at four years each. This same Eusebius reports another view as well, which I do not entirely reject (A), that most authorities extend the one [last] week of years to the sum of seventy years, reckoning each year as a ten-year period [reading the corrupt upputatio as supputatio]. They also claim that thirty-five years intervened between the passion of the Lord and the reign of Nero, and that it was at this latter date when the weapons of Rome were first lifted up against the Jews, this being the half-way point of the week of seventy years. After that, indeed, from the time of Vespasian and Titus (and it was right after their accession to power that Jerusalem and the temple were burned) up to the reign of Trajan another thirty-five years elapsed. And this, they assert, was the week of which the angel said to Daniel: "And he shall establish a compact with many for one week." For the Gospel was preached by the Apostles all over the world, since they survived even unto that late date. According to the tradition of the church historians, John the Evangelist lived up to the time of Trajan. Yet I am at a loss to know how we can understand the earlier seven weeks and the sixty-two weeks to involve seven years each, and just this last one to involve ten years for each unit of the seven, or seventy years in all.

So much for Eusebius. But Hippolytus has expressed the following opinion concerning these same weeks (B): he reckons the seven weeks as prior to the return of the people from Babylon, and the sixty-two weeks as subsequent to their return and extending to the birth of Christ. But the dates do not agree at all. If indeed the duration of the Persian Empire be reckoned at two hundred and thirty years, and the Macedonian Empire at three hundred, and the period thereafter up to the birth of the Lord be thirty years, then the total from the beginning of the reign of Cyrus, King of the Persians, until the advent of the Savior will be five hundred and sixty years. Moreover, Hippolytus places the final week at the end of the world and divides it into the period of Elias and the period of Antichrist, so that during the [first] three and a half years of the last week the knowledge of God is established. And as for the statement, "He shall establish a compact with many for a week" (Dan. 9:27), during the other three years under the Antichrist the sacrifice and offering shall cease. But when Christ shall come and shall slay the wicked one by the breath of His mouth, desolation shall hold sway till the end.

On the other hand Apollinarius of Laodicea in his investigation of the problem breaks away from the stream of the past and directs his longing desires towards the future, very unsafely venturing an opinion concerning matters so obscure. And if by any chance those of future generations should not see these predictions of his fulfilled at the time he set, then they will be forced to seek for some other solution and to convict the teacher himself of erroneous interpretation. And so, in order to avoid the appearance of slandering a man as having made a statement he never made, he makes the following assertion ---- and I translate him word for word: "To the period of four hundred and ninety years the wicked deeds are to be confined as well as all the crimes which shall ensue from those deeds. After these shall come the times of blessing, and the world is to be reconciled unto God at the advent of Christ, His Son. For from the coming forth of the Word, when Christ was born of the Virgin Mary, to the forty-ninth year, that is, the end of the seven weeks, [God] waited for Israel to repent. Thereafter, indeed, from the eighth year of Claudius Caesar [i.e., 48 A.D.] onward, the Romans took up arms against the Jews. For it was in His thirtieth year, according to the Evangelist Luke, that the Lord incarnate began His preaching of the Gospel (Luke 1) [sic!]. According to the Evangelist John (John 2 and 11), Christ completed two years over a period of three passovers. The years of Tiberius' reign from that point onward are to be reckoned at six; then there were the four years of the reign of Gaius Caesar, surnamed Caligula, and eight more years in the reign of Claudius. This makes a total of forty-nine years, or the equivalent of seven weeks of years. But when four hundred thirty-four years shall have elapsed after that date, that is to say, the sixty-two weeks, then [i.e. in 482 A.D.] Jerusalem and the Temple shall be rebuilt during three and a half years within the final week, beginning with the advent of Elias, who according to the dictum of our Lord and Savior (Luke 1) [sic!] is going to come and turn back the hearts of the fathers towards their children. And then the Antichrist shall come, and according to the Apostle [reading apostolum for apostolorum] he is going to sit in the temple of God (II Thess. 2) and be slain by the breath of our Lord and Savior after he has waged war against the saints. And thus, it shall come to pass that the middle of the week shall mark the confirmation of God's covenant with the saints, and the middle of the week in turn shall mark the issuing of the decree under the authority of Antichrist that no more sacrifices be offered. For the Antichrist shall set up the abomination of desolation, that is, an idol or statue of his own god, within the Temple. Then shall ensue the final devastation and the condemnation of the Jewish people, who after their rejection of Christ's truth shall embrace the lie of the Antichrist. Moreover, this same Apollinarius asserts that he conceived this idea about the proper dating from the fact that Africanus, the author of the Tempora [Chronology], whose explanation I have inserted above, affirms that the final week will occur at the end of the world. Yet, says Apollinarius, it is impossible that periods so linked together be wrenched apart, but rather the time-segments must all be joined together in conformity with Daniel's prophecy.

The learned scholar Clement, presbyter of the church at Alexandria, regards the number of years as a matter of slight consequence, asserting that the seventy weeks of years were completed by the span of time from the reign of Cyrus, King of the Persians, to the reign of the Roman emperors, Vespasian and Titus; that is to say, the interval of four hundred and ninety years, with the addition in that same figure of the two thousand three hundred days of which we made earlier mention. He attempts to reckon in these seventy weeks the ages of the Persians, Macedonians, and Caesars, even though according to the most careful computation, the number of years from the first year of Cyrus, King of the Persians and Medes, when Darius also bore rule, up to the reign of Vespasian and the destruction of the Temple amounts to six hundred and thirty.

When Origen came to deal with [reading praefuisset instead of profuisset] this chapter, he urged us to seek out what information we do not possess; and because he had no leeway for allegorical interpretation, in which one may argue without constraint, but rather was restricted to matters of historical fact, he made this brief observation in the tenth volume of the Stromata: "We must quite carefully ascertain the amount of time between the first year of Darius, the son of Ahasuerus, and the advent of Christ, and discover how many years were involved, and what events are said to have occurred during them. Then we must see whether we can fit these data in with the time of the Lord's coming."

We may learn what Tertullian had to say on the subject by consulting the book which he wrote against the Jews (Contra Judaeos), and his remarks may be set forth in brief: "How, then, are we to show that Christ came within the sixty-two (A) weeks? This calculation begins with the first year of Darius, since that was the time when the vision itself was revealed to Daniel. For he was told: 'Understand and conclude from (B) the prophesying of the command for me to give thee this reply. ...' Hence we are to commence our computation with the first year of Darius, when Daniel beheld this vision. Let us see, then, how the years are fulfilled up to the advent of Christ. Darius reigned nineteen years; Artaxerxes forty years; the Ochus who was surnamed Cyrus twenty-four years; (C) Argus, one year. Then Darius II, who was called Melas, twenty-one (D) years. Alexander the Macedonian reigned twelve years. And then after Alexander (who had ruled over both the Medes and the Persians, after he had conquered them, and had established his rule in Alexandria, calling it after his own name), Soter reigned (E) there in Alexandria for thirty-five years, and was succeeded by Philadelphus, who reigned for thirty-eight years (F). After him Euergetes reigned for twenty-five years, and then Philopator for seventeen years, followed by Epiphanes for twenty-four years. Furthermore the second Euergetes ruled for twenty (G) and nine years, and Soter for thirty-eight years. Ptolemy [sic!] for thirty-seven (H) years, and Cleopatra for twenty years and five months (I). Furthermore Cleopatra shared the rule with Augustus for thirteen years. After Cleopatra Augustus reigned forty-three years more. For all of the years of the reign of Augustus were fifty-six in number. And let us see (variant: we see) that in the forty-first year of the reign of Augustus, who ruled after the death of Cleopatra (J), Christ was born. And this same Augustus lived on for fifteen years after the time when Christ was born. And so the resultant periods of years up to the day of Christ's birth and the forty-first year of Augustus, after the death of Cleopatra [actually only twenty-nine years after Cleopatra's death ---- the language here is confusing], come to the total figure of four hundred and thirty-seven years and five months. This means that sixty-two and a half weeks were used up, or the equivalent of four hundred and thirty-seven years and six months, by the day when Christ was born. Then eternal righteousness was revealed, and the Saint of saints was anointed, namely Christ, and the vision and prophecy were sealed, and those sins were remitted which are allowed through faith in Christ's name to all who believe in Him." But what is the meaning of the statement that the "vision and prophecy are confirmed by a seal"? It means that all the prophets made proclamation concerning [Christ] Himself, saying that He was going to come and that He would have to suffer. Hence we read shortly thereafter in this Tertullian passage, "The years were fifty-six in number; furthermore, Cleopatra continued to reign jointly under Augustus...." It was because the prophecy was fulfilled by His advent that the vision was confirmed by a seal; and it was called a prophecy because Christ Himself is the seal of all the prophets, fulfilling as He did all that the prophets had previously declared concerning Him. Of course after His advent and His passion (variant; the passion of Christ), there is no longer any vision or prophecy (variant: or prophet) which declares that Christ will come [?]. And then a little later Tertullian says, "Let us see what is the meaning of (A) the seven and a half weeks, which in turn are divided up into a subsection of earlier weeks; by what transaction were they fulfilled? Well, after Augustus, (B) who lived on after Christ's birth, fifteen years elapsed. He was succeeded by Tiberius Caesar, and he held sway for twenty-two years, seven months and twenty-eight (C) days. In the fifteenth year of his reign (D) Christ suffered, being about thirty-three when He suffered. Then there was Gaius Caesar, also named Caligula, who reigned for three years, eight months and thirteen days. [Note that Claudius' reign of 13 years is here omitted.] Nero reigned for nine years, nine months and thirteen days. Galba ruled for seven months and twenty-eight (E) days; Otho for three months and five days; and Vitellius for eight months and twenty-eight (F) days. Vespasian vanquished the Jews in the first year of his reign, bringing the number of years to a total of fifty-two, plus six months. For he ruled for eleven years, and so by the date of his storming Jerusalem, the Jews had completed the seventy weeks foretold by Daniel."

As for the view which the Hebrews hold concerning this passage, I shall set it forth summarily and within a brief compass, leaving the credibility of their assertions to those who asserted them. And so let me put it in the form of a paraphrase (paraphrastikds) in order to bring out the sense more clearly. "O Daniel, know that from this day on which I now speak to thee (and that was the first year of the Darius who slew Belshazzar and transferred the Chaldean Empire to the Medes and Persians) unto the seventieth week of years (that is, four hundred and ninety years) the following events shall befall thy people in stages [literally: part by part]. First of all, God shall be appeased by thee in view of the earnest intercession thou hast just offered Him, and sin shall be canceled out and the transgression shall come to an end. For although the city at present lies deserted and the Temple lies destroyed to its very foundations [reading fundamenta for the non-existent frudamenta], so that the nation is plunged into mourning, yet within a fairly short time it shall be restored. And not only shall it come to pass within these seventy weeks that the city shall be rebuilt and the Temple restored, but also the Christ, who is the eternal righteousness, shall be born. And so shall the vision and the prophecy be sealed, with the result that there shall be no more any prophet to be found in Israel, and the Saint of saints shall be anointed. We read concerning Him in the Psalter: 'Because God, even Thy God, hath anointed Thee with the oil of gladness above thy fellows' (Ps. 44:8 =45:7). And in another passage He says of Himself: 'Be ye holy, for I also am holy' (Lev. 19:2). Know therefore that from this day on which I speak to thee and make thee the promise by the word of the Lord that the nation shall return and Jerusalem shall be restored, there shall be sixty-two weeks numbered unto the time of Christ the Prince and of the perpetual desolation of the Temple; and that there shall also be seven weeks in which the two events shall take place which I have already mentioned, namely that the nation shall return and the street shall be rebuilt by Nehemiah and Ezra. And so at the end of the weeks the decree of God shall be accomplished in distressing times, when the Temple shall again be destroyed, and the city taken captive. For after the sixty-two weeks the Christ shall be slain, and the nation who shall reject Him shall go out of existence" ---- or, as the Jews themselves put it, the kingdom of Christ which they imagined they would retain (G) shall not even be. And why do I speak of the slaying of Christ, and of the nation's utter forfeiture of God's help, since the Roman people were going to demolish the city and sanctuary under Vespasian, the leader who was to come? Upon his death the seven weeks or forty-nine years were complete, and after the city of Aelia was established upon the ruins of Jerusalem, Aelius Hadrian vanquished (H) the revolting Jews in their conflict with the general, Timus Rufus. It was at that time that the sacrifice and offering (ceased and) will continue to cease even unto the completion of the age, and the desolation is going to endure until the very end. We are not, say the Jews, greatly impressed by the fact that the seven weeks are mentioned first, and afterwards the sixty-two, and again a single week divided into two parts. For it is simply the idiomatic usage of the Hebrew language, as well as of antique Latin, that in quoting a figure, the small number is given first and then the larger. For example, we do not, according to good usage say in our language, "Abraham lived a hundred and seventy-five years"; on the contrary the Hebrews say, "Abraham lived five and seventy and one hundred years" (I). And so the fulfilment is not to follow the literal order of the words, but it shall be accomplished in terms of the whole sum, taken together. I am also well aware that some of the Jews assert that as for the statement about the single week, "He shall establish a covenant with many for one week," the division is between the reigns of Vespasian and Hadrian. According to the history of Josephus, Vespasian and Titus concluded peace with the Jews for three years and six month. And the [other] three years and six months are accounted for in Hadrian's reign, when Jerusalem was completely destroyed and the Jewish nation was massacred in large groups at a time, with the result that they were even expelled from the borders of Judaea. This is what the Hebrews have to say on the subject, paying little attention to the fact that from the first year of Darius, King of the Persians, until the final overthrow of Jerusalem, which befell them under Hadrian, the period involved is a hundred and seventy-four Olympiads or six hundred ninety-six years, which total up to ninety-nine Hebrew weeks plus three years ---- that being the time when Barcochebas, the leader of the Jews, was crushed and

Jerusalem was demolished to the very ground.

CHAPTER TEN

Verse 1. "In the third year of Cyrus, King of the Persians, a word was revealed unto Daniel, who was surnamed Belteshazzar, and it was a true word and great strength. For there is need of understanding in a vision." And how is it that we read at the end of the first vision, "And Daniel lived until the first year of Cyrus the King"? Well then, we understand that he enjoyed his former high position among the Chaldeans and was clothed in purple and fine linen right up until the first year of King Cyrus, when Cyrus overthrew the Chaldeans, and afterwards Daniel commenced service under Darius, the son of Ahasuerus of the Median line, who reigned over the kingdom of the Chaldeans. Or else, indeed, that Darius had already died in whose first year Daniel had learned of the mystery of the seventy weeks, and he is now relating that he beheld these things in the third year of King Cyrus. "And it was a true word and great strength" refers either to the strength of the God who was going to perform these things or to the strength of the prophet who would comprehend them.

Verses 2, 3. "In those days I, Daniel, mourned for the days of three weeks; I ate no desirable bread, and neither flesh or wine entered into my mouth; neither was I anointed with ointment until the days of three weeks were accomplished." By this example we are taught to abstain from the pleasanter types of food (I think that the term "desirable bread" is that inclusive) during a period of fasting, and that we neither eat flesh nor drink (A) wine, and especially that we desire no anointing with ointments. This custom is maintained among the Persians and Indians even to this day, that they use ointment as a substitute for baths. Also, Daniel afflicted his soul for three consecutive weeks, so that his intercession might not appear cursory or casual. By inference, indeed, we ought to make the observation that a person in mourning who bemourns the absence of one betrothed partakes of no desirable bread though it comes down from heaven itself; neither does he touch solid food, which is to be understood in the sense of meat, nor does he drink any wine, which gladdens the heart of man, or make his face cheerful with oil (as we read in the Psalms: "That he may make the face cheerful with oil" Ps. 103 [=104]: 15). By means of such a fast as this (B) the betrothed girl sheds tears which will be convincing, when her fiance has been taken from her. Daniel also did well to supplicate the Lord with boldness, inasmuch as in the first year of Cyrus's reign the captivity of the Jews had already been somewhat relaxed in its severity.

Verse 4. "And in the twenty-fourth day of the first month, I was beside the great river which is the Tigris." Ezekiel also had seen a great vision beside a river, the Chebar (Ez. 1). And it was by the stream of the Jordan that the heavens were opened to the gaze of our Lord and Savior and also to John the Baptist (Matt. 3). (C) Therefore those critics should leave off their foolish objections who raise questions about the presence of shadows and symbols in a matter of historical truth and attempt to destroy the truth itself by imagining that they should employ allegorical methods to destroy the historicity of rivers and trees and of Paradise [mentioned in Scripture].

Verse 5. "And I lifted my eyes and saw." We must lift up our eyes if we are to be able to discern a mystical vision.

"And behold, a person clothed in linen." Instead of "linen," as Aquila rendered it, Theodotion simply puts baddim [a mere transcription of the Hebrew word], whereas the Septuagint renders it as byssus [fine linen], and Symmachus as exaireta (choice vestments), (D), that is, "distinguished clothing" (praecipua). And instead of what we have rendered as, "Behold, a man," on the basis of the Hebrew text, Symmachus puts, "One like unto a man," inasmuch as he was not actually a man but only had the appearance of one.

"And his loins were girt about with pure gold." The Hebrew term for this is (E) 'wpz or ophaz [actually pointed as 'uwpaz in the Massoretic Text], a word which Aquila has rendered in this fashion: "And his loins were girt about with the color of ophax" [a Greek word which does not otherwise exist].

Verse 6. "And his body was like chrysolite." (F) For "chrysolite," one of the twelve gems inserted in the oracular breastplate of the high priest, the Hebrew has trs'ys (tharsis) [actually tarsiys or tarshish], a word which Theodotion and Symmachus simply left unchanged in transcription; but the Septuagint called it "the sea," according to the usage in the Psalms: "With a violent gale Thou dashest the ships of Tharsis in pieces," i.e., "the ships of the sea" (Ps. 47:8). Jonah, also, was desirous of fleeing, not to Tarsus, the Cilician city (as most people suppose), substituting one letter for another), nor to some region in India (as (G) Josephus imagines), but simply out to the high seas in general (Jonah 1).

Verse 7. "And I, Daniel, alone saw the vision, for the men who were with me saw it not; but an exceeding great terror fell upon them, and they fled away and hid themselves." The Apostle Paul had a similar experience in the Book of Acts, in that while the others could see nothing, he alone beheld the vision (Acts 22).

Verse 10. "And behold, a hand touched me, and lifted me up upon my knees. ..." The angel appeared in the form of a man and laid his hand upon the human prophet as he lay upon the ground, in order that he might not be terrified, beholding a form like his own.

Verse 11. "And he said to me, 'Daniel, thou man of desires. ...' " It was fitting that he be addressed as a man of desires, for by dint of urgent prayer and affliction of body and the discipline of severe fasting he desired to learn of the future and to be informed of the secret counsels of God. Instead of "man of desires," Symmachus rendered it as "desirable man." The term is apt, for every saint possesses a beauty of soul and is beloved by the Lord.

Verse 12. "And he said to me: 'Fear not, Daniel, for from the first day when thou didst set thine heart to understand and to afflict thyself in the sight of thy God (variant: thy Lord), thy words have been heard and granted, and I have come forth in response to thy words" (Vulgate: on account of thy words). On the twenty-fourth day of the first month, that is, of Nisan, after three weeks or twenty-one days had elapsed, he beheld this vision, and he heard from the angel that on the very first day he had begun to pray and to afflict himself before God, his words had been heard and granted. The question arises why, if he had been heard, was the angel not sent to him right away. Well, by reason of the delay an opportunity was afforded him of praying to the Lord at greater length, so that in proportion as his earnest desire was intensified, he might by his effort the more fully deserve to hear [or else: "might deserve to hear more, i.e., than he would otherwise"]. And as for the angel's statement, "And I have come in response to thy words," his meaning is this: "After thou didst begin to invoke God's mercy by good works and tearful supplication and fasting, then I for my part embraced the opportunity of entering in before God and praying for thee."

Verse 13. "But the prince of the kingdom of Persia withstood me for twenty-one days." In my opinion this was the angel to whose charge Persia was committed, in accordance with what we read in Deuteronomy: "When the Most High divided the nations and distributed the children of Adam abroad, then He established the bounds of the nations according to the number of the angels of God" (Deut. 32:8). These are the princes of whom Paul also says: "We speak forth among the perfect a wisdom which none of the princes of this world knew. For if they had known it, they would never have crucified the Lord of Glory" (I Cor. 2:6). And so the prince or angel of the Persians offered resistance, acting on behalf of the province entrusted to him, in order that the entire captive nation might not be released. And it may well be that although the prophet was graciously heard by God from the day when he set his heart to understand, the angel was nevertheless not sent to proclaim to him God's gracious decision, for the reason that the prince of Persia opposed him for twenty-one days, enumerating the sins of the Jewish people as a ground for their justly being kept in captivity and as proof that they ought not to be released.

"And behold, Michael, one of the chief princes, came to my assistance." That is, while the angel of the Persians was resisting thy petitions and my representations on thy behalf as I presented thy prayers to God, then there came to my assistance the angel Michael, who has oversight of the people of Israel. By chief princes we are of course to understand archangels.

"And I remained there close by the king of the Persians." He designates the angel or prince by the term "king of the Persians," and shows that he had tarried with Michael for a little as he spoke in opposition to the prince of the Persians.

Verse 14. "And I have come to teach thee what things shall befall thy people in the last days." The very petition which Daniel had requested is the thing which he deserves to hear from God, namely what is going to happen to the people of Israel, not in the near future, but in the last days, that is, at the end of the world.

Verse 16. (A) "O my lord, at the sight of thee my joints are loosed. ..." Theodotion interprets it this way, in accordance with what we read in the One Hundred and Second Psalm [i.e. the 103rd]: "Bless the Lord, O my soul, and all that is within me, bless His holy name." For our inward nature must direct its gaze without, before we deserve to behold a vision of God; and when we actually have beheld a vision of God, then our inward nature is converted within us and we become wholly of the number of those concerning whom it is written in another Psalm: "All the glory of the daughter of kings (B) is within, in golden borders" (Ps. 44:14).

Verse 19. "And as he spoke with me, I recovered strength and said, 'Speak, my Lord, for thou hast reassured me' And he said. ..." For unless the angel had reassured him by touching him like a son of man, so that his heart was freed of terror, he would not have been able to hearken to God's secrets. For that reason he now says, "Speak, for thou hast reassured me; for thou hast enabled me both to hear and understand what thou sayest."

Verse 20. " 'Dost thou know why I have come to thee? And now I will return to fight against the prince of the Persians.'" What he means is this: I have indeed come to teach thee of the things thou hast received in answer to prayer; but I am going to return once more to contend against the prince of the Persians in the sight of God, for he is unwilling that thy people be released from captivity.

"For (Vulgate: Therefore) as I was coming away, the prince of the Greeks appeared and entered in (Vulgate: and came up)." He means, "I myself was departing from God's presence in order to announce to thee [reading tibi for the inappropriate ubi] the events which are to befall thy people in the last days; and yet I am still not secure, since the prince of the Persians stands to plead against the granting of thy petitions and the acceptance of my advocacy on thy behalf. And behold, the prince of the Greeks, or Macedonians, had just come, and he entered in before God's presence to lodge accusation against the prince of the Medes and Persians, in order that the kingdom of the Macedonians might succeed in their place." Truly marvelous are the secret counsels of God, for it indeed came to pass that after the Jewish people had been freed from captivity, Alexander, king of the Macedonians, slew Darius and overthrew the kingdom of the Persians and Medes, so that the prince of the Greeks did overcome the prince of the Persians.

Verse 21. "Nevertheless I will relate to thee what has been set down in the Scripture of truth." That is, this is the order which the words follow. The fulfilment is still in doubt. For even though thou dost beseech the Lord and I present thy prayers to Him, yet the prince of the Persians takes his stand on the opposite side, and is unwilling that thy people be freed from captivity. But because the prince of the Greeks has come, and in the meantime is contending against the prince of the Persians, and also because I have Michael there as my assistant, I shall, during their mutual conflict, report to thee the coming events which God has foretold to me and has bidden me relate to thee. And let no one be disturbed by the question as to why mention is made of the prince of the Greeks or Hellenes rather than of the Macedonians, for Alexander, king of the Macedonians, did not take up arms against the Persians until he had first overthrown Greece and subjected it to his power.

"And no one is my helper in all these things except Michael, your prince." He implies, "I am that angel who presents thy prayers to God, and I have no other helper in petitioning God on your behalf except the archangel Michael, to whose charge the Jewish nation has been entrusted. And meanwhile the prince of the Greeks is engaged in a common effort with me at this particular time, contending against the prince of the Persians. We should review our ancient history and (A) consider whether by any chance that was the date of the conquest of the Persians by the Greeks. According to the Vulgate edition (of the Septuagint), this same vision is reckoned as extending to the end of the book, that is, the vision which appeared to Daniel in the third year of Cyrus, King of the Persians. On the other hand, according to the Hebrew original, the ensuing sections are separate from this, and recorded in an inverted order. The causes for this phenomenon we have already mentioned; that is, the matters here recorded are related as having occurred in the first year of the Darius who overthrew Belshazzar, not in the third year of Cyrus.

CHAPTER ELEVEN
Verse 1. "And from the first year of Darius the Mede, I stood up that he might be strengthened and confirmed." Daniel implies, "From the first year of the reign of Darius, who overthrew the Chaldeans and delivered me from the hand of my enemies to the extent of his ability (for even his sealing of the pit of lions with his signet ring was for my protection, lest my adversaries should slay me), I for my part stood before God, and I besought God's mercy upon him, in view of the man's love for me, in order that either he or his kingdom might be strengthened and confirmed. And since I persevered in my prayer, I was answered by God and given to understand the following information. After all, it is a customary thing with the prophets to bring in new speakers abruptly and without warning. So it is in Psalm Thirty-one [i.e., Thirty-two]: for when the prophet has petitioned God and said: "Thou art my refuge from my tribulation (B) which compassed me about; O Thou, who art my rejoicing, deliver me from

those who now encompass me," then God is abruptly brought in as the speaker, replying, "I will give thee understanding, and I will instruct thee in this way in which thou shalt go; I will fasten Mine eyes upon thee" (verses 7 and 8). So also here, as the prophet relates, "From the first year of Darius the Mede, I stood up and interceded that he might be strengthened and that his rule might be confirmed," God suddenly responds:

Verse 2. "And now I shall proclaim the truth to thee." And the meaning is this: "Because thou desirest to know what shall befall the kings of Persia, hearken thou to the order of events and hear the answer to thy request."

"And behold, three more kings shall arise in Persia, and the fourth shall be enriched exceedingly above them all, and when he shall have grown mighty through his wealth, he shall stir up all men against the kingdom of Greece." He states that four kings shall arise in Persia after Cyrus, namely Cambyses, the son of Cyrus, and the Magus named Smerdis, who married Pantaptes, the daughter of Cambyses. Then, when he was slain by seven Magi and Darius had succeeeded to his throne, the same Pantaptes married Darius, and by him gave birth to Xerxes, who became a most powerful and wealthy king, and led an innumerable host against Greece and performed those deeds which are related by the Greek historians. For in the archonship of Callias he destroyed Athens by fire, and about that same time waged the war at Thermopylae and the naval battle at Salamis. It was in his time that Sophocles and Euripides became famous [hardly Euripides, whose first play was given in 455, nine years after Xerxes' death], and Themistocles fled in exile to Persia, where he died as a result of drinking the blood of a bull. And so that writer is in error who records as the fourth king that Darius who was defeated by Alexander, for he was not the fourth king, but the fourteenth king of the Persians after Cyrus. It was in the seventh year of his rule that Alexander defeated and slew him. Moreover it should be observed that after he has specified four kings of Persia after Cyrus, the author [i.e., Daniel] omits the nine (C) others and passes right on to Alexander. For the Spirit of prophecy was not concerned about preserving historical detail but in summarizing only the most important matters.

Verses 3, 4. "But there shall rise up a strong king and shall rule with great power, and he shall do whatever he pleases. And when he shall have arisen, his kingdom shall be broken." He clearly refers to Alexander the Great, king of the Macedonians, and son of Philip. For after he had overcome the Illyrians and Thracians, and had conquered Greece and destroyed Thebes, he crossed over into Asia. And when he had routed Darius's generals and taken the city of Sardis, he afterwards captured India and founded the city of Alexandria. And then, when he had attained the age of thirty-two and the twelfth year of his reign, he died of poison.

"And it shall be divided towards the four winds of heaven, but not unto his own posterity nor according to his power with which he had borne rule." After Alexander his kingdom was divided towards the four winds, namely to the east, the west, the south, and the north. In Egypt, that is in the south, Ptolemy the son of Lagos was the first to become king. In Macedonia, that is in the west, the Philip who was also called Aridaeus, a brother of Alexander, became king. The king of Syria and Babylon and the remoter regions, that is, the east, was Seleucus Nicanor. Antigonus was king of Asia Minor and Pontus and of the other provinces in that whole area, that is, in the north. So much for the various regions of the world as a whole; but from the standpoint of Judea itself, the north would be Syria and the south would be Egypt. And as for the statement, "But not unto his own posterity," the implication is that Alexander would have no children, but rather, his kingdom would be rent asunder and fall to others who were not of his family, except of course for Philip, who kept Macedonia. Nor would it be according to the power of him who had borne rule, for the kingdom became feebler by division into four parts, for they constantly fought among themselves and raged with internecine fury.

"For his kingdom shall be rent in pieces (variant: destroyed), and that too among strangers besides these." Besides the four kingdoms of Macedonia, Asia Minor, Syria, and Egypt, the kingdom of the Macedonians was torn asunder among other rulers of less prominence and among petty kings. The reference here is to Perdiccas and Craterus and Lysimachus, for Cappadocia, Armenia, Bithynia, Heracleia, Bosphorus and various other provinces withdrew themselves from the Macedonian power and set up various kings for themselves.

Verse 5. "And the king of the South shall be strengthened." The reference is to Ptolemy, son of Lagos, who was the first to become king in Egypt, and was a very clever, mighty and wealthy man, and possessed such power that he was able to restore Pyrrhus, King of Epirus, to his kingdom after he had been driven out, and also to seize Cyprus and Phoenicia. And after he had conquered Demetrius, the son of Antigonus, he restored to Seleucus that portion of his kingdom which Antigonus had taken away from him. He also acquired Caria and many islands, cities, and districts unnecessary to detail at this time. But no further notice is taken of the other kingdoms, Macedonia and Asia Minor, because Judaea lay in a midway position and was held now by one group of kings and now by another. And it is not the purpose of Holy Scripture to cover external history apart from the Jews, but only that which is linked up with the nation of Israel.

"And one of his princes shall prevail over him, and he shall rule with great power, for his dominion shall be great." The person mentioned is Ptolemy Philadelphus, the second king of Egypt and the son of the former Ptolemy. It was in his reign that the Seventy (Septuaginta) translators are said to have translated the Holy Scripture into Greek. He also sent many treasures to Jerusalem for the high priest Eleazar, and votive vessels for the Temple. The curator of his library was Demetrius of Phalerum, a man of reputation among the Greeks as an orator and philosopher. Philadelphus is reported [reading narratur instead of the inappropriate narrantur] to have possessed such great power as to surpass his father Ptolemy. For history relates that he possessed two hundred thousand infantrymen, twenty thousand cavalry, and even two thousand chariots and four hundred elephants, which he was the first to import from Ethiopia. He also had a thousand five hundred war galleys of the type now known as Liburnian, and a thousand others for the transporting of military provisions. So great was his treasure of gold and silver that he received a yearly revenue from Egypt amounting to fourteen thousand eight hundred talents of silver, as well as grain in the amount of five or ten hundred thousand artabae (a measure containing three and a half modii [a modius being about three and a half pecks]).

Verse 6. "And at the end of the years they shall be leagued together (or, as Theodotion renders: And after his years they shall be united). And the daughter of the king of the South shall come to the king of the North in order to make friendship, but she shall not obtain strength of arm nor shall her seed endure. And she herself shall be handed over, as well as her young men (Vulgate: youths) who brought her and who were strengthening her in (these) times." As we have already said, it was Seleucus, surnamed Nicanor, who first ruled over Syria. The second king was Antiochus, who was called Soter. The third was Antiochus himself, who was called Theos, that is the Divine. He was the one who waged numerous wars with Ptolemy Philadelphus, who was the second ruler in Egypt, and he also fought with all the Babylonians and the men of the East, And so after many years Ptolemy Philadelphus wished to have done with this vexatious struggle, and so he gave his daughter, named Berenice, in marriage to Antiochus, who had already had by a previous wife, named Laodice, two sons, namely Seleucus, surnamed Callinicus, and the other, Antiochus. And Philadelphus conducted her as far as Pelusium and bestowed countless thousands of gold and silver by way of a dowry, from which circumstance he acquired the nickname of phernophoros or Dowry-giver (dotalis). But as for Antiochus, even though he had said he would regard Berenice as his royal consort and keep Laodice in the status of a concubine, he was finally prevailed upon by his love for Laodice to restore her to the status of queen, along with her children. But she was fearful that her husband might in his fickleness restore Berenice to favor once more, and so she had him put to death by her servants with the use of poison. And she handed over Berenice and the son whom she had born by Antiochus to Icadio and Genneus, princes of Antiochus, and then set up her elder son, Seleucus Callinicus, as king in his father's place. And so this is the matter referred to in this passage, namely that after many years Ptolemy Philadelphus and Antiochus Theos would conclude a friendship, and the daughter of the king of the South, that is Ptolemy, would go to the king of the North, that is Antiochus, in order to cement friendly relations between her father and her husband. And the text says that she will not be able to gain her end, nor shall her posterity remain upon the throne of Syria, but instead both Berenice and the men who had escorted her thither shall be put to death. And also the king, Antiochus, who had strengthened her, that is, through whom she could have obtained the mastery, was killed by his wife's poison.

Verses 7-9. "And a plant of the bud of her roots shall arise, and he shall come with an army and shall invade the province of the king of the North. And he shall abuse them and shall prevail. And he shall also carry away captive into Egypt their gods and their sculptures and their precious vessels of gold and silver; he shall prevail against the king of the North. And the king of the South shall enter into the kingdom and shall return to his own land." After the murder of Berenice and the death of her father, Ptolemy Philadelphus, in Egypt, her brother, who was also named Ptolemy and surnamed Euergetes, succeeded to the throne as the third of his dynasty, being in fact an offshoot of the same plant and a bud of the same root as she was, inasmuch as he was her brother. He came up with a great army and advanced into the province of the king of the North, that is Seleucus Callinicus, who together with his mother Laodice was ruling in Syria, and abused them, and not only did he seize Syria but also took Cilicia and the remoter regions beyond the Euphrates and nearly all of Asia as well. And then, when he heard that a rebellion was afoot in Egypt, he ravaged the kingdom of Seleucus and carried off as booty forty thousand talents of silver, and also precious vessels and images of the gods to the amount of two and a half thousand. Among them were the same images which Cambyses had brought to Persia at the time when he conquered Egypt. The Egyptian people were indeed devoted to idolatry, for when he had brought back their gods to them after so many years, they called him Euergetes (Benefactor). And he himself retained possession of Syria, but he handed over Cilicia to his friend, Antiochus, that he might govern it, and the provinces beyond the Euphrates he handed over to Xanthippus, another general.

Verse 10. "And his sons shall be provoked, and they shall assemble a multitude of great armies, and he shall come with haste like a flood. And he shall return and be stirred up, and he shall join battle with his army." After the flight and death of Seleucus Callinicus, his two sons, the Seleucus surnamed Ceraunus and the Antiochus who was called the Great, were provoked by a hope of victory and of avenging their father, and so they assembled an army against Ptolemy Philopator and took up arms. And when the elder brother, Seleucus, was slain in Parygia in the third year of his reign through the treachery of Nicanor and Apaturius, the army which was in Syria summoned his brother, Antiochus the Great, from Babylon to assume the throne. And so this is the reason why the present passage states that the two sons were provoked and assembled a multitude of very sizable armies. But it implies that Antiochus the Great came by himself from Babylon to Syria, which at that time was held by Ptolemy Philopator, the son of Euergetes and the fourth king to rule in Egypt. And after he had successfully fought with his generals, or rather had by the betrayal of Theodotius obtained possession of Syria (which had already been held by a succession of Egyptian kings), he became so emboldened by his contempt for Philopator's luxurious manner of life and for the magical arts which he was said to employ, that he took the initiative in attempting an invasion of Egypt itself.

Verses 11, 12. "And the king of the South, being provoked, shall go forth and shall prepare an exceeding great multitude, and a multitude shall be given into his hand. And he shall take a multitude, and his heart shall be lifted up, because (Vulgate: and) he shall cast down many thousands. But he shall not prevail." The Ptolemy surnamed Philopator, having lost Syria through the betrayal of Theodotius, gathered together a very great multitude and launched an invasion against Antiochus the Great, who now bears the title of king of the North, at the region where Egypt borders upon the province of Judaea. For owing to the nature of the region, this locality lies partly to the south and partly to the north. If we speak of Judaea, it lies to the north of Egypt and to the south of Syria. And so when he had joined battle near the town of Raphia at the gateway of Egypt, Antiochus lost his entire army and was almost captured as he fled through the desert. And after he had conceded the loss of Syria, the conflict was finally brought to an end upon the basis of a treaty and certain conditions of peace. And this is what the Scripture means here by the statement that Ptolemy Philopator "shall cast down many thousands" and yet shall not prevail. For he was unable to capture his adversary. The sequel now follows.

Verses 13, 14. "And the king of the North shall return and shall prepare a much greater multitude than before, and in the end of times and years he shall come in haste with a large army and great resources. And in those times many shall rise up against the king of the South." This indicates that Antiochus the Great, who despised the worthlessness of Ptolemy Philopator (for he had fallen desperately in love with a lute-player named Agathoclea and also her brother, retaining Agatho-cles himself as his concubine and afterwards appointing him as general of Egypt), assembled a huge army from the upper regions of Babylon. And since Ptolemy Philopator was now dead, Antiochus broke his treaty and set his army in motion against Philopator's four-year-old son, who was called Epiphanes. For so great was the dissoluteness and arrogancy of Agathoclea, that those provinces which had previously been subjected to Egypt rose up in rebellion, and even Egypt itself was troubled with seditions. Moreover Philip, King of Macedon, and Antiochus the Great made peace with each other and engaged in a common struggle against Agathocles and Ptolemy Eprphanes, on the understanding that each of them should annex to his own dominion those cities of Ptolemy which lay nearest to them. And so this is what is referred to in this passage, which says that many shall rise up against the king of the South, that is, Ptolemy Epiphanes, who was then a mere child.

"Moreover the children of the transgressors of thy people shall lift themselves up, that they may fulfil the vision, and then fall to ruin (Vulgate: and they shall fall to ruin)." During the conflict between Antiochus the Great and the generals of Ptolemy, Judaea, which lay between them, was rent into contrary factions, the one group favoring Antiochus, and the other favoring Ptolemy. Finally the high priest, Onias, fled to Egypt, taking a large number of Jews along with him, and was given by Ptolemy an honorable reception. (A) He then received the region known as Heliopolis, and by a grant of the king, he erected a temple in Egypt like the temple of the Jews, and it remained standing up until the reign of Vespasian, over a period of two hundred (B) and fifty years. But then the city itself (C), which was known as the City of Onias, was destroyed to the very ground because of the war which the Jews had subsequently waged against the Romans. There is consequently no trace of either city or temple now remaining. But as we were saying, countless multitudes of Jews fled to Egypt on the occasion of Onias's pontificate, and the land was filled with a large number from Cyrene as well. For Onias affirmed (A) that he was fulfilling the prophecy written by Isaiah: "There shall be an altar of the Lord in Egypt, and the name of the Lord shall be found in their territories" (Isa. 19:19). And so this is the matter referred to in this passage: "The sons of the transgressors of thy people," who forsook the law of the Lord and wished to offer blood-sacrifices to God in another place than what He had commanded. They would be lifted up in pride and would boast that they were fulfilling the vision, that is, the thing which the Lord had enjoined. But they shall fall to ruin, for both temple and city shall be afterwards destroyed. And while Antiochus held Judaea, a leader of the Ptolemaic party called Scopas (B) Aetholus was sent against Antiochus, and after a bold campaign he took Judaea and took the aristocrats of Ptolemy's party back to Egypt with him on his return.

Verses 15, 16. "And the king of the North shall come, and shall cast up a mound and capture the best fortified cities, and the arms of the South shall not withstand. And his chosen ones shall rise up to resist, and they shall have no strength. And he shall come upon him and do according to his own desire, and there shall be none to stand against his face. And he shall stand in the glorious land and it shall be consumed by his hand." Purposing to retake Judaea and the many cities of Syria, Antiochus joined battle with Scopas, Ptolemy's general, near the sources of the Jordan near where the city now called Paneas was founded, and he put him to flight and besieged him in Sidon together with ten thousand of his soldiers. In order to free him, Ptolemy dispatched the famous generals, Eropus, Menocles and Damoxenus (Vulgate: Damoxeus). Yet he was unable to lift the siege, and finally Scopas, overcome by famine, had to surrender and was sent away with his associates, despoiled of all he had. And as for the statement, "He shall cast up a mound," this indicates that Antiochus is going to besiege the garrison of Scopas in the citadel of Jerusalem for a long time, while the Jews add their exertions as well. And he is going to capture other cities which had formerly been held by the Ptolemaic faction in Syria, Cilicia and Lycia (variant: Lydia). For at that time Aphrodisias, Soloe, Zephrion, Mallos, Anemurium (variant: Anemurum), Selenus, Coracesium, Coricus, Andriace, Lymira, Patara (variant: Patra), Xanthus, and finally Ephesus were all captured. These things are related by both Greek and Roman historians. And as for the statement, "And he shall stand in the glorious land, and it shall be consumed (or, finished) by his hand," the term "glorious land," or, as the Septuagint interprets it, "the land of desire" (that is, in which God takes pleasure) signifies Judaea, and particularly Jerusalem, to which Antiochus pursued those men of Scopas's party who had been honorably (C) received there. Instead of the phrase, "glorious land," as Aquila rendered it, Theodotion simply puts the Hebrew word itself, (D) Sabin; instead of that Symmachus translated it "land of bravery."

Verses 17-19. "And he shall set his face to come and possess all his kingdom, and he shall make upright conditions with him. And he shall give him the daughter of women, that she may overthrow him" (Vulgate: it). That is to say, the intention is to overthrow him, that is, Ptolemy, or else to overthrow it, that is, his kingdom. Antiochus not only wished to take possession of Syria, Cilicia, and Lycia, and the other provinces which had belonged to Ptolemy's party, but also to extend his empire to Egypt. He therefore used the good offices of Eucles of Rhodes to betroth his daughter, Cleopatra, to young Ptolemy in the seventh year of his reign; and in his thirteenth year she was given to him in marriage, professedly endowed with all of Coele-syria and Judaea as her marriage-portion. By pleonasm she is called a daughter of women, just as the poet says:

. . .Thus she spake with her mouth.
. . .And with these ears did I drink in her voice.

[The second line is quoted from Vergil's Aeneid, iv, 359; the first line I have not been able to locate; neither seems to be particularly appropriate to the context.]

"And she shall not stand, neither shall she be for him. And he shall turn his face to the islands and shall capture many; and she shall cause the prince of her reproach to cease, and his reproach shall be turned upon him. And he shall turn his face to the empire of his own land; and he shall stumble and fall, and shall not be found." For he was unable to take possession of Egypt, because Ptolemy Epiphanes and his generals detected the strategem and followed a cautious policy. And besides, Cleopatra inclined more to her husband's side than to her father's. And so he turned his attention to Asia Minor, and by carrying on naval warfare against a large number of islands, he seized Rhodes, Samos, Colophon (variant: Colophonia and Bocla), Phocea and many other islands. But he was opposed by Lucius Scipio Nasica and also his brother, Publius Scipio Africanus, who had vanquished Hannibal. For since the consul Nasica, the brother of Africanus, was of a somewhat sluggish disposition, the Roman senate was unwilling to entrust to him a war against so mighty a king as Antiochus. Africanus therefore offered to assume the post of deputy on a voluntary basis, in order to obviate any damage that his brother might cause. Consequently Antiochus was vanquished and commanded to confine his rule to the other side of the Taurus range. And so he took refuge in Apamia and Susa and advanced to the easternmost cities of his realm [reading regni for regi]. And during a war against the Elymaeans he was destroyed together with his entire army. And so this is what the Scripture refers to in this passage, when it states that he would capture many islands, and yet because of the Roman conqueror he would lose the kingdom of Asia, and that the disgrace he had inflicted would come back upon his own head; and that in the end he would flee from Asia Minor and return to the empire of his own land, and would then stumble and fall, so that his place would not be found.

Verse 20. "And there shall stand up in his place one most vile and unworthy of kingly honor, and in a few days he shall be destroyed, not in rage nor in a battle." The reference is to the Seleucus surnamed Philopator, the son of Antiochus the Great, who during his reign performed no deeds worthy of Syria or of his father, but perished ingloriously without fighting a single battle. Porphyry, however, claims that it was not this Seleucus who is referred to, but rather Ptolemy Epiphanes, who contrived a plot against Seleucus and prepared an army to fight against him, with the result that Seleucus was poisoned by his own generals. They did this because when someone asked Seleucus where he was going to get the financial resources for the great enterprises he was planning, he answered that his financial resources consisted in his friends. When this remark was publicly noised abroad, the generals became apprehensive that he would deprive them of their property and for that reason did him to death by nefarious means. Yet how could Ptolemy be said to rise up in the place of Antiochus the Great, since he did nothing of the sort? This is especially improbable since the Septuagint translated: "And there shall stand up a plant from his root," that is, "of his issue and seed," who should deal a severe blow to the prestige of the empire; "and within a few days he shall be destroyed without wrath or battle." The Hebrews claim that it is Trypho who was intended by the man who was most vile and unworthy of kingly honor, for as the boy-king's guardian he seized the throne for himself.

Verse 24. "And there shall stand up in his place one despised, and the kingly honor shall not be given him; and he shall come privately and shall obtain the kingdom by fraud. And the arms of the fighter shall be overcome before his face and shall be broken, and the prince of the covenant as well. And after friendly advances he shall deal deceitfully with him, and shall go up and shall overcome with a small people. And he shall enter into rich and prosperous cities, and shall do things which his fathers never did, nor his fathers' fathers. He shall scatter their spoil and their booty and their wealth, and shall undertake plots against the best fortified cities, and shall continue thus for a time." Up to this point the historical order has been followed, and there has been no point of controversy between Porphyry and those of our side (variant: and us). But the rest of the text from here on to the end of the book he interprets as applying to the person of the Antiochus who was surnamed Epiphanes, the brother of Seleucus and the son of Antiochus the Great. He reigned in Syria for eleven years after Seleucus, and he seized Judaea, and it is under his reign that the persecution of God's Law is related, and also the wars of the Maccabees. But those of our persuasion believe all these things are spoken prophetically of the Antichrist who is to arise in the end time. But this factor appears to them as a difficulty for our view, namely the question as to why the prophetic discourse should abruptly cease mention of these great kings and shift from Seleucus to the end of the world. The answer is that in the earlier historical account where mention was made of the Persian kings, only four kings of Persia were presented, following after Cyrus, and many who came in between were simply skipped over, so as to come quickly to Alexander, king of the Macedonians. We hold that it is the practice of Scripture not to relate all details completely, but only to set forth what seems of major importance. Those of our school insist also that since many of the details which we are subsequently to read and explain are appropriate to the person of Antiochus, he is to be regarded as a type of the Antichrist, and those things which happened to him in a preliminary way are to be completely fulfilled in the case of the Antichrist. We hold that it is the habit of Holy Scripture to set forth by means of types the reality of things to come, in conformity with what is said of our Lord and Savior in the Seventy-first [i.e Seventy-second] Psalm, a psalm which is noted at the beginning as being Solomon's, and yet not all the statements which are made concerning can be applied to Solomon. For certainly he neither endured "together with the sun and before the moon from generation to generation," nor did he hold sway from sea to sea, or from the River unto the ends of the earth; neither did all the nations serve him, nor did his name endure before the sun; neither were all the tribes of earth blessed in him, nor did all races magnify him. But in a partial way these things were set forth in advance, by shadows as it were, and by a mere symbol of the reality, in the person of Solomon, in order that they might be more perfectly fulfilled in our Lord and Savior. And so, just as the Savior had Solomon and the other saints as types of His advent, so also we should believe that the Antichrist very properly had as a type of himself the utterly wicked king, Antiochus, who persecuted the saints and defiled the Temple. Let us therefore follow along with the explanation point by point, and let us briefly observe in the case of each item what it signifies to those of the other school of thought and what it signifies to those of our school, in accordance with each of the two explanations. Our opponents say that the one who was to "stand up in the place of" Seleucus was his brother, Antiochus Epiphanes. The party in Syria who favored Ptolemy would not at first grant him the kingly honor, but he later secured the rule of Syria by a pretense of clemency. And as Ptolemy fought and laid everything waste, his arms were overcome and broken before the face of Antiochus. Now the word arms implies the idea of strength, and therefore also the host of any army is known as a hand [i.e. manus, "hand," may also signify a "band of armed men"]. And not only does the text say that he conquered Ptolemy by fraud, but also the prince of the covenant he overcame by treachery, that is, Judas Maccabaeus. Or else this is what is referred to, that after he had secured peace with Ptolemy and he had become the prince of the covenant, he afterwards devised a plot against him. Now the Ptolemy meant here was not Epiphanes, who was the fifth Ptolemy to reign in Egypt, but Ptolemy Philometor, the son of Antiochus' sister, Cleopatra; and so Antiochus was his maternal uncle. And when after Cleopatra's death Egypt was ruled by Eulaius, the eunuch who was Philometor's tutor, and by Leneus, and they were attempting to regain Syria, which Antiochus had fraudulently seized, warfare broke out between the boy Ptolemy and his uncle. And when they joined battle between Pelusium and Mt. Casius, Ptolemy's generals were defeated. But then Antiochus showed leniency towards the boy, and making a pretense of friendship, he went up to Memphis and there received the crown after the Egyptian manner. Declaring that he was looking out for the lad's interests, he subjected all Egypt to himself with only a small force of men, and he entered into rich and prosperous cities. And so he did things which his father had never done, nor his fathers' fathers. For none of the kings of Syria had ever laid Egypt waste after this fashion and scattered all their wealth. Moreover he was so shrewd that he even overcame by his deceit the well-laid plans of those who were the boy-king's generals. This is the line of interpretation which Porphyry followed, pursuing the lead of (A) Sutorius with much redundancy, discoursing of matters which we have summarized within a brief compass. But the scholars of our viewpoint have made a better and correcter interpretation, stating that the deeds are to be performed by the Antichrist at the end of the world. It is he who is destined to arise from a small nation, that is from the Jewish people, and shall be so lowly and despised that kingly honor will not be granted him. But by means of intrigue and deception he shall secure the government and by him shall the arms of the fighting nation of Rome be overcome and broken. He is to effect this result by pretending to be the prince of the covenant, that is, of the Law and Testament of God. And he shall enter into the richest of cities and shall do what his fathers never did, nor his fathers' fathers. For none of the Jews except the Antichrist has ever ruled over the whole world. And he shall form a design against the firmest resolves of the saints and shall do everything [he wishes] for a time, for as long as God's will shall have permitted him to do these things.

Verses 25, 26. "And his strength and his heart shall be stirred up against the king of the South with a great army. And the king of the South shall be aroused to war with many and very strong auxiliary forces; and they shall not stand, for they shall form designs against him. And they that eat bread with him shall destroy him, and his army shall be crushed, and many shall fall down slain." Porphyry interprets this as applying to Antiochus, who set forth with a great army on a campaign against his sister's son. But the king of the South, that is the generals of Ptolemy, were also roused to war with many and very powerful auxiliary forces, but they could not stand against the fraudulent schemes of Antiochus. For he pretended to be at peace with his sister's son and ate bread with him, and afterwards he took possession of Egypt. But those of our view with greater plausibility interpret all this as applying to the Antichrist, for he is to be born of the Jewish people and come from Babylon, and is first of all going to vanquish the king of Egypt, who is one of the three horns of which we have already spoken earlier.

Verses 27----30. "And the heart of the two kings shall be to do evil, and they speak falsehood at one table, and they shall not prosper, because as yet the end is unto another time. And he shall return into his land with much riches." There is no doubt but what Antiochus did conclude a peace with Ptolemy and ate at the same table with him and devised plots against him, and yet without attaining any success thereby, since he did not obtain his kingdom but was driven out by Ptolemy's soldiers. But it cannot be proved from this set of facts that the statement of this Scripture was ever fulfilled by past history, namely that there were two kings whose hearts were deceitful and who inflicted evil upon each other. Actually, Ptolemy was a mere child of tender years and was taken in by Antiochus' fraud; how then could he have plotted evil against him? And so our party insist that all these things (A) refer to the Antichrist and to the king of Egypt whom he has for the first time overcome.

"And his heart shall be against the holy covenant, and he shall succeed and return into his own land. At the time appointed he shall return and shall come to the South; but the latter time shall not be like the former. And the galleys shall come upon him, and the Romans, and he shall be dealt a heavy blow." Or, as another has rendered it, "... and they shall threaten him with attack." Both the Greek and the Roman historians relate that after Antiochus had been expelled from Egypt and had gone back once more, he came to Judaea, that is, against the holy covenant, and that he despoiled the Temple and removed a huge amount of gold; and then, having stationed a garrison in the citadel, he returned to his own land. And then two years later he gathered an army against Ptolemy and came to the South. And while he was besieging his two nephews, the brothers of Ptolemy and sons of Cleopatra, at Alexandria, some Roman envoys arrived on the scene, one of whom was Marcus (B) Popilius Laenas. And when he had found Antiochus standing on the shore and had conveyed the senatorial decree to him by which he was ordered to withdraw from those who were friends of the Roman people and to content himself with his own domain, then Antiochus delayed his reply in order to consult with his friends. But Laenas is said to have made a circle in the sand with the staff which he held in his hand, and to have drawn it around the king, saying, "The senate and people of Rome give order for you to make answer in this very spot as to what your decision is." At these words Antiochus was greatly alarmed and said, "If this is the good pleasure of the senate and people of Rome, then I must withdraw." And so he immediately set his army in motion. But he is said to have been dealt a heavy blow, not that he was killed but that he lost all of his proud prestige. As for the Antichrist, there is no question but what he is going to fight against the holy covenant, and that when he first makes war against the king of Egypt, he shall straightway be frightened off by the assistance (C) of the Romans. But these events were typically prefigured under Antiochus Epiphanes, so that this abominable king who persecuted God's people foreshadows the Antichrist, who is to persecute the people of Christ. And so there are many (D) of our viewpoint who think that Domitius Nero [actually Domitius was the name of Nero's father, Ahenobarbus] was the Antichrist because of his outstanding savagery and depravity.

"And he shall return and shall be angry at the covenant of the sanctuary, and he shall succeed; and he shall return and take thought concerning (Vulgate: against) those who have abandoned the covenant of the sanctuary." We read of these matters at greater length in the exploits of the Maccabees (I Macc. 1), where we learn that after the Romans expelled him from Egypt, he came in anger against the covenant of the sanctuary and was welcomed by those who had forsaken the law of God and taken part in the religious rites of the Gentiles. But this is to be more amply fulfilled under the Antichrist, for he shall become angered at the covenant of God and devise plans against those whom he wishes to forsake the law of God. And so Aquila has rendered in a more significant way: "And he shall devise plans to have the compact of the sanctuary abandoned."

Verse 31. "And arms shall stand on his part, and they shall defile (Vulgate: that (?) they may defile) the sanctuary of strength, and they shall take away the continual sacrifice, and shall place there the abomination unto desolation." Instead of "arms," (E) another writer has rendered it as "seed," so as to imply descendants and progeny. But those of the other viewpoint claim that the persons mentioned are those who were sent by Antiochus two years after he had plundered the Temple in order to exact tribute from the Jews, and also to eliminate the worship of God, setting up an image of Jupiter Olympius in the Temple at Jerusalem, and also statues of Antiochus himself. These are described as the abomination of desolation, having been set up when the burnt offering and continual sacrifice were taken away. But we on our side contend that all these things took place in a preliminary way as a mere type of the Antichrist, who is destined to seat himself in the Temple of God, and make himself out to be as God. The Jews, however, would have us understand these things as referring, not to Antiochus Epiphanes or the Antichrist, but to the Romans, of whom it was earlier stated, "And war galleys shall come," whether Italian or Roman, "and he shall be humbled." Considerably later, says the text, a king, Vespasian, shall emerge from the Romans themselves, who had come to Ptolemy's assistance and threatened Antiochus. It is his arms or descendants who would rise up, namely his son Titus, who with his army would defile the sanctuary and remove the continual sacrifice and devote the temple to permanent desolation. By the terms siim (Siyyim) and chethim (Kittiym), which we have rendered as "galleys" and "Romans," the Jews would have us understand "Italians" and "Romans."

Verse 32. "And ungodly men shall deceitfully dissemble against the covenant. But the people who know their God shall prevail and succeed." And in Maccabees we read that there were some who, to be sure, pretended that they were custodians of God's law, and later they came to terms with the Gentiles; yet the others adhered to their religion. But in my opinion this will take place in the time of the Antichrist, when the love of many shall wax cold. It is concerning these people that our Lord says in the Gospel, "Dost thou think that the Son of man, when He comes, will find faith upon the earth?" (Luke 18:8).

Verse 33. "And they that are learned among the people shall teach many and they shall fall by the sword and by fire and by captivity and by spoil for many days." The books of Maccabees relate the great sufferings the Jews endured at the hands of Antiochus and they stand as a testimony of their triumph; for they endured fire and sword, slavery and rapine, and even the ultimate penalty of death itself for the sake of guarding the law of God. But let no one doubt that these things are going to happen under the Antichrist, when many shall resist his authority and flee away in various directions. The Jews, of course, interpret these things as taking place at the destruction of the Temple, which took place under Vespasian and Titus, and they claim that there were very many of their nation who knew their Lord and were slain for keeping His law.

Verses 34, 35. "And when they shall have fallen, they shall be relieved with a small help; and many shall be joined to them deceitfully. And some of the learned shall fall, that they may be refined as by fire and that they may be chosen and made white even to the time before appointed, because there shall yet be another time." Porphyry thinks that the "little help" was Mattathias of the village of (variant: mountain of) Modin, for he rebelled against the generals of Antiochus and attempted to preserve the worship of the true God (I Macc. 2). He says he is called a little help because Mattathias was slain in battle; and later on his son Judas, who was called Maccabaeus, also fell in the struggle; and the rest of his brothers were likewise taken in by the deceit of their adversaries. Consult the books of Maccabees for the details. And all these events took place, he asserts, for the purpose of testing and choosing out the saints, that they might be made white until the time before appointed, inasmuch as victory was deferred until another time. Our writers, however, would have it understood that the small help shall arise under the reign of the Antichrist, for the saints shall gather together to resist him, and afterwards a great number of the learned shall fall. And this shall take place in order that they may be refined as by fire in the furnace, and that they may be made white and may be chosen out, until the time before determined arrives ---- for the true victory shall be won at the coming of Christ. Some of the Jews understand these things as applying to the princes Severus and Antoninus, who esteemed the Jews very highly. But others understand the Emperor Julian as the one referred to; for after they had been oppressed by Gaius Caesar and had steadfastly endured such suffering in the afflictions of their captivity, Julian rose up as one who pretended love for the Jews, promising that he would even offer sacrifice in their temple. They were to enjoy a little help from him, and a great number of the Gentiles were to join themselves to their party, although falsely and insincerely. For it would only be for the sake of their own idolatrous religion that they would pretend friendship to the Jews. And they would do this in order that those who were approved might be made manifest. For the time of their true salvation and help will be the coming of the Christ; for the Jews mistakenly imagine (A) that he (i.e., their Messiah) is yet to come, for they are going to receive the Antichrist (when he comes) (I Cor. 11).

Verse 36. "And the king shall do according to his will, and he shall be lifted up and shall magnify himself against every god; and he shall speak arrogant words against the God of gods, and shall manage successfully until the wrath be accomplished (Vulgate: indignation); for the determination is made." Or else, as another has translated it: "for in him shall be the consummation." The Jews believe that this passage has reference to the Antichrist, alleging that after the small help of Julian a king is going to rise up who shall do according to his own will and shall lift himself up against all that is called god, and shall speak (B) arrogant words against the God of gods. He shall act in such a way as to sit in the Temple of God and shall make himself out to be God, and his will shall be prospered until the wrath of God is fulfilled, for in him the consummation will take place. We too understand this to refer to the Antichrist. But Porphyry and the others who follow his lead suppose the reference to be to Antiochus Epiphanes, pointing out that he did raise himself up against the worship of God, and pushed his arrogance so far as to command his own statue to be set up in the Temple in Jerusalem. And as for the subsequent statement, "And he shall manage successfully until the wrath be accomplished, for the consummation shall be in him," they understand it to mean that his power will endure until such time as God becomes angry at him and orders him to be killed.

For indeed Polybius and Diodorus, who composed the histories of the (C) Bibliothecae (Libraries), relate that Antiochus not only took measures against the God of Judaea, but also was impelled by an all-consuming avarice to attempt the plunder of the temple of (D) Diana in Elymais, because it was so wealthy. But he was so beset by the temple guard and the neighboring populace, and also by certain fearful apparitions, that he became demented and finally died of illness. And the historians record that this befell him because he had attempted to plunder the temple of Diana. But we for our part maintain that even though this thing befell him, it did so because he had perpetrated great cruelty upon the saints of God and had defiled His Temple. For we ought not to suppose that it was because of something he only attempted to do but from which he then desisted by an act of repentance, but rather because of something he actually did he was punished.

Verses 37-39. "And he shall make no account of the god of his fathers, and he shall be engrossed in lust for women; nor shall he have regard for any of the gods, for he shall rise up against everything. But he shall worship the god Maozim in his place, and a god which his fathers knew not shall he worship with gold and silver and precious stones and things of great price. And he shall take measures to fortify Maozim, together with a strange god whom (A) he has acknowledged. And he shall increase glory and shall grant them power over many and shall divide the land as a free gift." Instead of our rendering, the Septuagint translates: "...and he will not be subject to the lusts of women." And again, instead of "the god Maozim (m'dym) [the Massoretic text has md'uzziym]," as the Hebrew has it, Aquila renders, "the God of mighty powers (fortitudinum)," whereas the Septuagint says, "the most mighty God." But because there is an ambiguity of position in the Hebrew original of the phrase we rendered by, "And he shall be engrossed in lust for women," Aquila renders it simply word for word (in Greek): "And he shall have no understanding with regard to the god of his fathers, and (B) in regard to the desire of women and in regard to every god he shall have no understanding"; that is (in Latin): "And concerning the god of his fathers he shall not understand, and concerning the lust for women, and concerning every god he shall not understand." There are two interpretations current concerning these words, that he cherished lust for women, and that he cherished no lust for them. If we read it one way and understand it as an apo koinou [the use of a common word in two different clauses]: "And he shall have no knowledge concerning a lust for women," then it is more easily applied to the Antichrist; i.e., that he will assume a pretense of chastity in order to deceive many. But if we read it in this fashion: "And occupied with lust for women," understanding, "...he shall be," then it is more appropriate to the character of Antiochus. For he is said to have been an egregious voluptuary, and to have become such a disgrace to the dignity of kingship through his lewdness and seductions, that he publicly had intercourse with actresses and harlots, and satisfied his sexual passions in the presence of the people. As for the god Maozim, Porphyry has offered an absurd explanation, asserting that Antiochus's generals set up a statue of Jupiter in the village of Modin, from which came Mattathias and his sons; moreover they compelled the Jews to offer blood-sacrifices to it, that is, to the god of Modin. The next statement, "...and he shall worship a god whom his fathers did not know" is more appropriate to the Antichrist than to Antiochus. For we read that Antiochus held to the religion of the idols of Greece and compelled the Jews and Samaritans to worship his own gods. Likewise in regard to the statement, "...and he shall take measures to fortify Maozim, together with a strange god whom he has acknowledged; and he shall increase glory and grant them power over many, and shall divide the land as a free gift," Theodotion has interpreted as follows: "And he shall conduct these affairs so as to fortify garrisons with a strange god, and with them he shall manifest and increase glory; and he shall cause them to bear rule over many and divide up the land as a free gift." Symmachus rendered it "refuges" instead of "garrisons." Porphyry explained this as meaning that the man is going to fortify the citadel in Jerusalem and will station garrisons in the rest of the cities, and will instruct the Jews to worship a strange god, which doubtless means Jupiter. And displaying the idol to them, he will persuade them that they should worship it. Then he will bestow upon the deluded both honor and very great glory, and he shall deal with the rest who have borne rule in Judaea, and apportion estates unto them in return for their falsehood, and shall distribute gifts. The Antichrist likewise is going to make lavish bestowal of many rewards upon those whom he has deceived, and will divide up the land to his soldiery. And those whom he will not be able to subject to himself by fear he will subject through their cupidity.

Verses 40, 41. "And at the predetermined time the king of the South shall war against him, and the king of the North shall come against him like a tempest with chariots, with horsemen and with a great navy; and he shall invade lands and destroy them and pass through. And he shall enter into the glorious land, and many shall fall." Theodotion rendered: ". . .and many shall be enfeebled." And according to Aquila, the many that fell are to be understood as cities or districts or provinces. This too is referred by Porphyry to Antiochus, on the ground that in the eleventh year of his reign he warred for a second time against his nephew, Ptolemy Philometor. For when the latter heard that Antiochus had come, he gathered many thousands of soldiery. But Antiochus invaded many lands like a mighty tempest, with his chariots and horsemen and large navy, and laid everything waste as he passed through. And he came to the glorious land, that is, Judaea, which Symmachus rendered as "land of strength." In place of this Theodotion used the Hebrew word itself, Sabai (variants: Sabam and Saba) (sby). And Antiochus used the ruins of the wall of the city to fortify the citadel, and thus he continued on his way to Egypt. But those of our viewpoint refer these details also to the Antichrist, asserting that he shall first fight against the king of the South, or Egypt, and shall afterwards conquer Libya and Ethiopia, for these constitute the three broken horns about which we read previously. And then he shall come to the land of Israel, and many cities or provinces shall be given into his hands.

"And only these cities shall be saved from his hands: Edom, Moab, and the principality of the children of Ammon." They say that in his haste to fight Ptolemy, the king of the South, Antiochus left untouched the Idumaeans, Moabites, and Ammonites, who dwelt to the side of Judaea, lest he should make Ptolemy the stronger by engaging in some other campaign. The Antichrist also is going to leave Idumaea, Moab, and the children of Ammon (i.e., Arabia) untouched, for the saints are to flee thither to the deserts.

Verses 42, 43. "And he shall lay his hand upon the lands, and the land of Egypt shall not escape; and he shall have power over the treasures of gold and of silver, and over all the precious things of Egypt. And likewise he shall pass through [reading transibit for transivit] the Libyans (Vulgate: Libya and Ethiopia) and the Ethiopians." We read that Antiochus partially accomplished this. But as for the added detail, "He shall pass through the Libyans and Ethiopians," our school insists that this is more appropriate to the Antichrist. For Antiochus never held Libya, which most writers understand to be North Africa, nor Ethiopia; unless, of course, his capture of Egypt involved the harrassment of those provinces of Egypt which lay in the same general region as Ethiopia, and which lay as distant neighbors to it, on the other side of the deserts. Hence there is no assertion of his conquering them, but only the statement that he passed through the Libyans and the Ethiopians.

Verses 44, 45. "And tidings from the East and from the North shall trouble him. And he shall come thither with a great host to destroy and slay very many. And he shall pitch his tent in Apedno between (A) the two seas, upon the famous and holy mountain; and he shall come even unto its summit, and none shall help him." Even for this passage Porphyry has some nebulous application to Antiochus, asserting that in his conflict with the Egyptians, Libyans, and Ethiopians, passing through them he was to hear of wars which had been stirred up against him in the North and the East. Thence he was to turn back and overcome the resistance of the Aradians [Aradus was an island off the coast of Phoenicia], and lay waste the entire province along the coastline of Phoenicia. And then he was to proceed without delay against Artaxias, the king of Armenia, who was moving down from the regions of the East, and having slain a large number of his troops, he would pitch his tent in the place called Apedno which is located between the two broadest rivers, the Tigris and the Euphrates. But it is impossible to state upon what famous and holy mountain he took his seat, after he had proceeded to that point. After all, it cannot be shown that he took up his seat between two seas, and it would be foolish to interpret the two seas as being the two rivers of Mesopotamia. But Porphyry gets around this famous mountain by following the rendering of Theodotion, who said: ". . .upon the sacred Mount Saba between the two seas." And even though he supposes that Saba was the name of a mountain in Armenia or Mesopotamia, he cannot explain why it was holy. [The Massoretic text has the common noun, sebiy, which means "beauty" or "honor," and gives no room for any proper noun, Saba.] To be sure, if we assume the right of making things up, we can add the detail which Porphyry fails to mention, that the mountain, forsooth, was called holy, because it was consecrated to idols in conformity with the superstition of the Armenians. The account then says: "And he shall come even unto the summit of that same mountain," ---- supposedly in the province of Elam, which is the easternmost Persian area. And there when he purposed to plunder the temple of Diana, which contained countless sums of money, he was routed by the barbarians, for they honored that shrine with a remarkable veneration. And Antiochus, being overcome with grief, died in Tabes, a town in Persia. By use of a most artificial line of argument Porphyry has concocted these details as an affront to us; but even though he were able to prove that these statements applied to Antiochus instead of the Antichrist, what does that matter [reading quid instead of the inappropriate qui] to us? For do we not on the basis of all the passages of Scripture prove the coming of Christ and the falsehood of the Antichrist? For assume that these things did refer to Antiochus, what injury does that inflict upon our religious faith? Is it not true that in the earlier vision also, which contained a prophecy fulfilled in Antiochus, there is some reference to the Antichrist? And so let Porphyry banish his doubts and stick to manifest facts. Let him explain the meaning of that rock which was hewn from the mountain without hands, and which grew to be a great mountain and filled the earth, and which smashed to pieces the fourfold image. And let him say who that Son of man is who is going to come with clouds and stand before the Ancient of Days and have bestowed upon him a kingdom which shall never come to an end, and who is going to be served by all [reading omnes for omnem] nations, tribes, and language-groups. Porphyry ignores these things which are so very clear and maintains that the prophecy refers to the Jews, although we are well aware that they are to this very day in a state of bondage. And he claims that the person who composed the book under the name of Daniel made it all up in order to revive the hopes of his countrymen. Not that he was able to foreknow all of future history, but rather he records events that had already taken place. Thus Porphyry confines himself to false claims in regard to the final vision, substituting rivers for the sea, and positing a famous and holy mountain, Apedno (B) even though he is unable to furnish any historical source in which he has read about it. Those of our party, on the other hand, explain the final chapter of this vision as relating to the Antichrist, and stating that during his war against the Egyptians, Libyans, and Ethiopians, in which he shall smash three of the ten horns, he is going to hear that war has been stirred up against him in the regions of the North and East. Then he shall come with a great host to crush and slay many people, and shall pitch his tent in Apedno near Nicopolis, which was formerly called Emmaus, at the beginning of the mountainous region in the province of Judaea. Finally he shall make his way thence to go up to the Mount of Olives and ascend to the area of Jerusalem; and this is what the Scripture means here: "And when he has pitched his tent...." at the foothills of the mountainous province between two seas. These are, of course, that which is now called the Dead Sea on the east, and the Great Sea on the shore of which lie Caesarea, Joppa, Ashkelon, and (C) Gazae. Then he shall come up to the summit thereof, that is of the mountainous province, or the apex of the Mount of Olives, which of course is called famous because our Lord and Savior ascended from it to the Father. And no one shall be able to assist the Antichrist as the Lord vents his fury upon him. Our school of thought insists that Antichrist is going to perish in that spot from which the Lord ascended to heaven. Apedno is a compound word, which upon analysis yields the meaning of "his throne" (the Greek thronou autou), or (in Latin) "thy throne" [or, if tui is a misprint for sui, his throne]. And the meaning is that he shall pitch his tent (D) and his throne between the seas upon the famous, holy mountain. Symmachus translated this passage as follows (in Greek): "And he shall stretch out the tents of his stable between the seas in the holy mountain of power, and he shall come even unto its height"; which means in Latin: "And he shall stretch forth the pavilions of his cavalry between the seas, upon the holy mountain of power, and shall come even unto the apex of the mountain." Theodotion renders it: "And he shall pitch his tent in (A) Aphedanum between the seas in the holy Mount Saba, and he shall come to the region thereof." Aquila says: "And he shall set up the tent of his headquarters in (Greek) Aphadanon between the seas, in the glorious, holy mountain, and he shall come even unto its border." Only the Septua-gint frees itself from the problem about the name by translating: "And he shall establish his tent between the seas and the holy mountain of desire and he shall come to the hour of his final end." Adhering to this rendering, Apollinarius omits all mention of the name Apedno. I have gone into this matter at some length not only for the purpose of exposing Porphyry's misrepresentation (for either he was ignorant of all these matters or else he pretended not to know them) but also to show the difficulty in Holy Scripture. And yet men who altogether lack experience lay special claim to understanding it apart from the grace of God and the scholarship of preceding generations. Now it should be observed that Hebrew has no letter P, but uses instead the letter phe, which has the force of the Greek phi. [An interesting observation, but rather puzzling. Ordinarily the Hebrew pe is spirantized only after a vowel sound, and is hard the rest of the time. It is hard and doubled in this particular word, 'appadnow, according to the Massoretic pointing.] It is simply that in this particular place the Hebrews write the letter (B) phe, yet it is to be pronounced as p. But that the Antichrist is going to come to the summit of the holy, famous mountain and perish there is a fact upon which Isaiah expatiates more fully, saying: "The Lord shall in the holy mountain cast down the face of the ruler of the darkness which is over all races, and him who rules over all peoples, and the (C) anointing which is applied against (variant: with which he was anointed against) all the nations." [This rather incoherent quotation varies very considerably from Jerome's own rendering of Isaiah 25:7 in the Vulgate, and also from the Septuagint rendering. The editors were apparently so dubious about it that they failed to give the citation at all.]

CHAPTER TWELVE

Verses 1-3. "But at that time shall Michael rise up, the great prince, who stands for the children of thy people, and a time shall come such as never occurred from the time that nations began to exist even unto that time. And at that time shall thy people be saved, even everyone who shall be found written in the book. And many of those who sleep in the dust of the earth shall awake, some unto life everlasting, and others unto reproach, that they may behold it always. But those who are instructed shall shine as the brightness of the firmament; and they that instruct many as to righteousness, as the stars for all eternity." Up until this point Porphyry somehow managed to maintain his position and impose upon the credulity of the naive [reading imperitis for imperitus] among our adherents as well as the poorly educated among his own. But what can he say of this chapter, in which is described the resurrection of the dead, with one group being revived for eternal life and the other group for eternal disgrace? He cannot even specify who the people were under Antiochus who shone like the brightness of the firmament, and those others who shone like the stars for all eternity. But what will pigheadedness not resort to? Like some bruised serpent, he lifts up his head as he is about to die, and pours forth his venom upon those who are themselves at the point of death. This too, he declares, was written with reference to Antiochus, for after he had invaded Persia, he left his army with Lysias, who was in charge of Antioch and Phoenicia, for the purpose of warring against the Jews and destroying their city of Jerusalem. All these details are related by Josephus, the author of the history of the Hebrews. Porphyry contends that the tribulation was such as had never previously occurred, and that a time came along such as had never been from the time that races began to exist even unto that time. But when victory was bestowed upon them, and the generals of Antiochus had been slain, and Antiochus himself had died in Persia, the people of Israel experienced salvation, even all who had been written down in the book of God, that is, those who defended the law with great bravery. Contrasted with them were those who proved to be transgressors of the Law and sided with the party of Antiochus. Then it was, he asserts, that these guardians of the Law, who had been, as it were, slumbering in the dust of the earth and were cumbered with a load of afflictions, and even hidden away, as it were, in the tombs of wretchedness, rose up once more from the dust of the earth to a victory unhoped for, and lifted up their heads, rising up to everlasting life, even as the transgressors rose up to everlasting disgrace. But those masters and teachers who possessed a knowledge of the Law shall shine like the heaven, and those who have exhorted the more backward peoples to observe the rites of God shall blaze forth after the fashion of the stars for all eternity. He also adduces the historical account concerning the Maccabees, in which it is said that many Jews under the leadership of Mattathias and Judas Maccabaeus fled to the desert and hid in caves and holes in the rocks, and came forth again after the victory (I Macc. 2.) These things, then, were foretold in metaphorical language as if it concerned a resurrection of the dead. But the more reasonable understanding of the matter is that in the time of the Antichrist there shall occur a tribulation such as there has never been since nations began to exist. For assume that Lysias won the victory instead of being defeated, and that he completely crushed the Jews instead of their conquering; certainly such tribulation would not have been comparable to that of the time when Jerusalem was captured by the Babylonians, the Temple was destroyed, and all the people were led off into captivity. And so after the Antichrist is crushed and destroyed by the breath of the Savior's mouth, the people written in God's book shall be saved; and in accordance with the merits of each, some shall rise up unto eternal life and others unto eternal shame. But the teachers shall resemble the very heavens, and those who have instructed others shall be compared to the brightness of the stars. For it is not enough to know wisdom unless one also instructs others; and the tongue of instruction which remains silent and edifies no one else can receive no reward for labor accomplished. This passage is expressed by Theodo-tion and the Vulgate edition [of the Septuagint] in the following fashion: "And those who understand shall shine forth like the radiance of the firmament, and many of the righteous like the stars forever and ever." Many people often ask whether a learned saint and an ordinary saint shall both enjoy the same reward and one and the same dwelling-place in heaven. Well then, the statement is made here, according to Theodotion's rendering, that the learned will resemble the very heavens, whereas the righteous who are without learning are only compared to the brightness of the stars. And so the difference between learned godliness and mere godly rusticity shall be the difference between heaven and the stars.

Verse 4. "But Thou, O Daniel, shut up the words and seal the book, even to the time appointed. Many shall pass over, and knowledge shall be manifold." He who had revealed manifold truth to Daniel now signifies that the things he has said are matters of secrecy, and he orders him to roll up the scroll containing his words and set a seal upon the book, with the result that many shall read it and inquire as to its fulfilment in history, differing in their opinions because of its great obscurity. And as for the statement, "Many shall pass over" or "go through," this indicates that it will be read by many people. For it is a familiar expression to say: "I have gone through a book," or, "I have passed through an historical account." Indeed this is the idea which Isaiah also expressed in regard to the obscurity of his own book: "And the sayings of that book shall be like the words of a book that is sealed. And if they shall give it to an illiterate man, saying, 'Read it,' he will reply, 'I do not know how to read.' But if they give it to a man who does know how to read and say, 'Read the book,' he will reply, 'I cannot read it, because it is sealed up' " (Isa. 39:11). Also in the Revelation of John, there is a book seen which is sealed with seven seals inside and outside. And when no one proves able to break its seals, John says, "I wept sore; and a voice came to me, saying, 'Weep not: behold the Lion of the tribe of Judah, the Root of David, has prevailed to open the book and break its seals' " (Rev. 5:4). But that book can be opened by one who has learned the mysteries of Scripture and understands its hidden truths, and its words which seem dark because of the greatness of the secrets they contain. He it is who can interpret the parables and transmute the letter which killeth into the spirit which quickeneth.

Verses 5, 6. "And I Daniel looked, and behold as it were two other persons were standing, one on this side upon the river-bank, and the other upon that side, on the other bank of the river. And I said to the man that was clothed in linen, that stood upon the waters of the river, 'How long shall it be to the end of these wonders?'" Daniel saw two angels standing on either side upon the bank of the river of Babylon. Although it is mentioned here without specifying its name, I suppose that in line with the preceding vision it would be the Tigris River, which is called Eddecel (H-d-q-l) in Hebrew. Yet Daniel does not address his question to those who were standing upon either bank, but rather to the one whom he had seen at the beginning, who was clothed in vesture of linen or byssus, which is called baddim (b-d-y-m) in Hebrew. And this same angel was standing upon the waters of the river of Babylon, treading upon them with his feet. From this fact we understand that the former pair of angels whom he saw standing upon the bank and did not question or deem worthy of interrogation were the angels of the Greeks and Persians. But this first angel was the gracious one who had presented Daniel's prayers before God during the twenty-one days while the angel of the Persians was opposing him. And Daniel was asking him (variant: asks him) about these wonders spoken of in the present vision, as to the time when they should be accomplished. Porphyry, of course, assigns this time to the period of Antiochus, after his usual fashion, whereas we assign it to the time of Antichrist.

Verse 7. "And I heard the man that was clothed in linen, that stood upon the waters of the river: when he had lifted up his right hand and his left hand to heaven and had sworn by Him that liveth forever, that it should be unto a time and times and half a time." Porphyry interprets a time and times and half a time to mean three and a half years; and we for our part do not deny that this accords with the idiom of Sacred Scripture. For we read in an earlier section that seven times passed over Nebuchadnezzar, that is, the seven years of his existence as a wild beast. The expression was also used in the vision of the four beasts, the lion, the bear, the leopard, and the other beast whose name was not specified but which represented the kingdom of the Romans. Right afterwards the statement is made concerning the Antichrist that (A) he will humble kings and utter speeches against the Exalted One and will crush the saints of the

Most High; moreover he will imagine that he can alter times and laws. And the saints shall be turned over to his power unto a time and times and half a time. And the court will sit for judgment, in order that power may be removed and utterly broken and vanish away until the very end. And clearly the reference is to the coming of Christ and the saints when it is said: "But kingdom and power and the greatness of the kingdom which lies beneath the whole heaven shall be bestowed upon the people of the saints of the Most High, whose kingdom is an everlasting kingdom; and all the kings shall serve and obey Him." If therefore the earlier references which were plainly written concerning the Antichrist are assigned by Porphyry to Antiochus and to the three and a half years during which he asserts the Temple was deserted (cf. Verse 1, above), then he is under obligation to prove that the next statement, "His kingdom is eternal, and all kings shall serve and obey him," likewise pertains to Antiochus, or else (as he himself conjectures) to the people of the Jews. But it is perfectly apparent that such an argument will never stand. We read in the books of Maccabees----and Josephus also concurs in the same opinion (Book 11, chap. 10) ---- that the Temple in Jerusalem lay defiled for three years, and under Antiochus Epiphanes an idol of Jupiter stood within it (B); that is to say, from Chislev, the ninth month, of the one hundred forty-fifth year of the Macedonian rule until the ninth month of the one hundred forty-eighth year, which amounts to three years. But under the Antichrist it is not stated that the desolation and overthrow of the holy Temple shall endure for three years, but for three years and a half, that is, one thousand two hundred and ninety days.

"And when the scattering of the band of the holy people shall be accomplished, all these things shall be fulfilled." When it is stated that the people of God shall have been scattered ---- either under the persecution of Antiochus, as Porphyry claims, or of Antichrist, which we deem to be closer to fact ---- at that time shall all these things be fulfilled.

Verses 8-10. "And I heard, and understood not. And I said, 'O my lord, what shall happen after these things?' And he said, 'Go, Daniel, for the words are shut up and sealed until the time (C) of the end. Many shall be chosen and made white and shall be tried as fire; and the wicked shall deal wickedly. And none of the wicked shall understand, but the learned shall understand.'" The prophet wished to comprehend what he had seen, or rather, what he had heard, and he desired to understand the reality of the things to come. For he had heard of the various wars of kings, and of battles between them, and a detailed narrative of events; but he had not heard the names of the individual persons involved. And if the prophet himself heard and did not understand, what will be the case with those men who presumptuously expound a book which has been sealed, and that too unto the time of the end, a book which is shrouded with many obscurities? But he comments that when the end comes, the ungodly will lack comprehension, whereas those who are learned in the teaching of God will be able to understand. "For wisdom will not enter the perverted soul, nor can it impart itself to a body which is subject to sins." [The editors do not cite the source of this quotation.]

Verse 11. "And from the time that the continual sacrifice shall be taken away, and the abomination unto desolation shall be set up, there shall be a thousand two hundred and ninety days." Porphyry asserts that these one thousand two hundred and ninety days were fulfilled in the desolation of the Temple in the time of Antiochus, and yet both Josephus and the Book of Maccabees, as we have said before, record that it lasted for only three years. From this circumstance it is apparent that the three and a half years are spoken of in connection with the time of the Antichrist, for he is going to persecute the saints for three and a half years, or one thousand two hundred and ninety days, and then he shall meet his fall on the famous, holy mountain. And so from the time of the removal of the endelekhismos, which we have translated as "continual sacrifice," i.e., the time when the Antichrist shall obtain possession of the world (variant: the city) and forbid the worship (A) of God, unto the day of his death the three and a half years, or one thousand two hundred and ninety days, shall be fulfilled.

Verse 12. "Blessed is he that waiteth and cometh unto a thousand three hundred and thirty-five days." He means that he is blessed who waits for forty-five days beyond the predetermined number, for it is within that period that our Lord and Savior is to come in His glory. But the reason for the forty-five days of inaction after the slaying of the Antichrist is a matter which rests in the knowledge of God; unless, of course, we say that the rule of the saints is delayed in order that their patience may be tested. Porphyry explains this passage in the following way, that the forty-five days beyond the one thousand two hundred and ninety signify the interval of victory over the generals of Antiochus, or the period when Judas Maccabaeus fought with bravery and cleansed the Temple and broke the idol to pieces, offering blood-sacrifices in the Temple of God. He might have been correct in this statement if the Book of Maccabees had recorded that the Temple was polluted over a period of three and a half years instead of just three years (I Macc. 4).

Verse 13. "But thou, (B) Daniel, go thy way until the time appointed, and take thy rest (Vulgate: thou shalt rest) and thou shalt stand in thy lot unto the end of the days." Instead of this Theodotion translated it: "But go thy way and take thy rest, and thou shalt rise up again in thy turn at the end of the days." From this remark it is demonstrated that the whole context of the prophecy has to do with the resurrection of all the dead, at the time when the prophet also is to rise. And it is vain for Porphyry to claim that all these things which were spoken concerning the Antichrist under the type of Antiochus actually refer to Antiochus alone. As we have already mentioned, these false claims have been answered at greater length by Eusebius of Caesarea, Apollinarius of Laodicea, and partially also by that very able writer, the martyr Methodius; and anyone who knows of these things can look them up in their writings. (C) Thus far we have been reading Daniel in the Hebrew edition; but the remaining matter to the end of the book has been translated from Theodotion's edition.

CHAPTER THIRTEEN

Verses 1, 2. "Now there was a man that dwelt in Babylon whose name was Joakim; and he took a wife whose name was Susanna, the daughter of Helcias, a very beautiful woman and one who feared the Lord" (Vulgate: God). Having expounded to the best of my ability the contents of the book of Daniel according to the Hebrew, I shall briefly set forth the comments of Origen concerning the stories of Susanna and of Bel contained in the Tenth Book of his Stromata. These remarks are from him (D) and one may observe them in the appropriate sections (i.e., of Origen's work).

Verse 3. "And being righteous folk, her parents had educated their daughter in conformity with the law of Moses (Vulgate: because they were righteous, they had instructed....)" This verse should be used as a testimony in order to urge parents to teach their daughters in accordance with God's law and holy Word, as well as their sons.

Verse 5. "And there were (E) two of the elders of the people (the Vulgate omits: of the people) who were appointed judges that year." There was a Jew who used to allege that these men were Ahab and Zedekiah (variant: Alchias and Zedekiah), of whom Jeremiah wrote: "The Lord do to thee as Ahab and Zedekiah, whom the king of Babylon roasted in the fire because of the iniquity they had wrought in Israel and because they had committed adultery (variant: were committing adultery) with the wives of their citizens" (Jer. 29). [In Jer. 21:23; 29:21 they are mentioned as Ahab, the son of Koliah, and Zedekiah, the son of Maaseiah, two false prophets who were denounced by Jeremiah.]

"It was concerning them that the Lord said that iniquity came forth from Babylon on the part of the ancient judges who appeared to govern the people. They used to frequent the house of Joakim...." Very appropriately it is not said of these sinful elders, "They governed the people," but rather, "They appeared to govern." For those who furnish good leadership to the people are the ones who govern them, but those who merely have the title of judge and lead the people unjustly only appear to govern the people rather than actually doing so.

Verse 8. "And they were inflamed with lust (F) for her, and they perverted their own mind and turned their eyes away that they might not look toward heaven nor remember just judgments." What the Greeks call pathos we render more correctly by "emotion" than by "passion." And so it was this emotion, this lustful desire, which aroused or even smote the hearts of the elders. But in order that they might lay some basis for it in their hearts and might plan how to satisfy their desires, they perverted their own minds. And as their minds were subverted, they turned away their eyes that they might not regard heavenly things or remember righteous judgments, or God, or honor, or character, the factors for good which are inherent in all men. "And behold, Susanna was taking a walk according to her custom." [This is Verse 13 according to the Septuagint, not according to Theodotion, who does not include the verse at all.] It has been stated already that Susanna was actually in the habit of taking walks in the mornings. For the sake of pleasing those people who seek out Scriptural precedent for everything we do, it would not be inappropriate to seize upon this passage about taking walks, and say that it is a good thing for a person to take walks for the invigorating of his body. Origen says that he has taken this particular passage from the Septuagint; by this statement he shows that he has not discussed the rest of the chapter on the basis of the Septuagint translation.

Verse 19. [Vulgate: XIII:22] "Susanna sighed and said: 'I am straitened on every side '" Anyone who has attained to the acme of perfect virtue never says that she is faced with a crisis of decision, when she is unable to escape the hands of adulterers who say, "Consent to us and have intercourse with us; for otherwise, if thou art unwilling, we will witness against thee that a young man was with thee and thou sentest away thy maidens for this purpose." It is of course a characteristic of human frailty to fear a death which is inflicted upon one because of his uprightness. To be sure we might interpret her distress as arising not from the prospect of death but from the contumely and disgrace which would be heaped upon her by those accusers who would claim: "A young man was with her, and she sent away her maidens for that reason."

Verse 22. " 'For if I do this, it is death to me; but if I do not. ... .'" She speaks of sin as death. For just as in the case of one who commits adultery, the adultery means death, so also every sin which results in death is to be equated with death. And we believe we die as often as we sin unto death. And therefore on the other hand we rise again and are made alive just as often as we perform deeds which are worthy of life.

Verse 23. " 'But it is better for me to fall into your hands without doing the deed than to sin in the sight of the Lord.'" In the Greek the word is not hairetoteron, or "better" [actually: more preferable], but haireton, which we may render by "good" [more accurately: "preferable"]. And so she chose her words well when she avoided saying, "It is better for me to fall into the hands of my enemies, the elders, than to sin in the sight of the Lord"; for thus she avoided calling something better in comparison with sin, which was not a good thing at all. But, she remarks, it is good for me not to do the wicked thing, and to fall into your clutches without sinning in God's sight. Therefore one should not use the comparative and say, "It is better for me to fall into your clutches than to sin in God's sight," but rather the positive, "It is good for me not to do the wicked thing and fall into your clutches, rather than to commit sin in God's sight."

Verse 24. "And Susanna cried out with a great voice. ..." Her voice was great, not because of the intense vibrations it sent through the air nor because of the outcry that came from her lips, but because of the greatness of the chastity with which she called out to the Lord. And so for this reason the Scripture did not attribute a great voice to the outcry of the elders, for the following statement is merely: "The elders also cried out against her."

Verse 42. "But Susanna cried out with a great voice...." Her voice was rendered the clearer because of the emotion of her heart, the honest sincerity of her avowal, and the uprightness of her conscience. And so, although men would not listen to it, her outcry to God was great.

Verse 45. "And as she was being led away to die, the Lord raised up the holy spirit of a young boy." By this language it is shown that the Holy Spirit did not then enter into Daniel, but rather that He was already within him, and only because of the tenderness of his years He had remained inactive. Nor could He show forth His works until an occasion arose and the Lord stirred him up on behalf of the holy woman.

Verse 46. "And he cried out with a great voice: 'I am innocent of the blood of this woman. .. .'" Because the Holy Spirit was roused up within him and dictated to the boy what he should say, his voice was great. And if there is any place in Holy Scripture where the voice of a sinner is called great, it has (yet) to be noted.

Verses 54 ff. " 'Tell me under which tree thou sawest them conversing with each other.' And he answered, 'Under the mastic tree.' And Daniel said to him, 'Well hast thou lied against thine own head; for behold, the angel of God, having received His sentence from Him, shall cleave thee in twain.' And a little while later the other elder said, 'Under the holm tree.' And Daniel said to him, 'Well hast thou lied against thine own head; but the angel of the Lord waiteth with a sword to sever thee in twain.'" Since the Hebrews reject the story of Susanna, asserting that it is not contained in the Book of Daniel, we ought to investigate carefully the names of the trees, the skhinos and the prinos, which the Latins interpret as "holm-oak" and "mastic-tree," and see whether they exist among the Hebrews and what their derivation is ---- for example, as "cleavage" [Latin (scissio) is derived from "mastic" [Greek skhinos], and "cutting" or "sawing" [Latin sectio, serratio] is derived from "holm tree" [Greek prinos, which resembles the Greek word for "to saw": prio] in the language of the Greeks. But if no such derivation can be found, then we too are of necessity forced to agree with the verdict of those who claim that this chapter [Greek pericope] was originally composed in Greek, because it contains Greek etymology not found in Hebrew. [That is, because Daniel twice makes a sinister wordplay based upon the Greek names of these two trees, and a similar pun could not be made out from the Hebrew names, if any, of these trees, the story itself could never have been composed in Hebrew.] But if anyone can show (A) that the derivation of the ideas of cleaving and severing from the names of the two trees in question is valid in Hebrew, then we may accept this scripture also as canonical.

Verse 60. "And the whole congregation (Vulgate: assembly) cried out with a great voice and blessed God, who saveth those who trust in Him. ..." If the whole congregation put them to death, the view which we mentioned earlier is apparently refuted (A), namely that these were the elders Ahab and Zedekiah, in conformity with Jeremiah's statement (chap. 29). The only other possibility is that instead of taking the statement, "They killed them," literally, we interpret it as meaning that they gave them over to the king of Babylon to be put to death. That would be just like when we say that the Jews put the Savior to death; not that they smote Him themselves, but they gave Him over to be slain and cried out, "Crucify Him! Crucify Him!" (John 19:15).

Verse 63. "But Helcias and his wife praised God for their daughter Susanna. ..." Like true saints they praise God after a worthy fashion, not simply on the ground of Susanna's deliverance from the clutches of the elders ---- for that would hardly be sufficient matter for praise or of any decisive importance, even if she had not been so delivered ---- but rather on the ground that no immorality was found in her.

CHAPTER FOURTEEN

"And as soon as he had opened the door, the king looked upon the table and cried out with a great voice: 'Great art thou, O Bel, and there is no deceit with thee.'" The statement of Scripture in this passage, "He cried out with a great voice," may seem, because of its reference to an idolator ignorant of God, to refute the observation put forth a little previously, that the expression "great voice" is found only in connection with saints. This objection is easily solved by asserting that this particular story is not contained in the Hebrew of the Book of Daniel. If, however, anyone should be able to prove that it belongs (B) in the canon, then we should be obliged to seek out some answer to this objection.

www.ingramcontent.com/pod-product-compliance
Lightning Source LLC
Chambersburg PA
CBHW071116120626
46546CB00003B/1361